Vienna

Austria

KNOPF
CITY GUIDES

**THIS IS A BORZOI BOOK
PUBLISHED BY
ALFRED A. KNOPF, INC**

Copyright © 2000 Alfred A. Knopf
Inc., New York

ISBN 0-375-70657-7

Originally published in France by
Nouveaux Loisirs, a subsidiary of
Gallimard, Paris 1999, and in Italy
by Touring Editore, Srl.,
Milano 1999.
Copyright © 1999
Nouveaux Loisirs,
Touring Editore, Srl.

SERIES EDITORS
Seymourina Cruse and Marisa Bassi
BARCELONA EDITION:
Ædelsa Atelier Tourisme
GRAPHICS
Élizabeth Cohat, Yann Le Duc
LAYOUT:
Silvia Pecora
MINI- MAPS:
Fiammetta and Flavio Badalato
BARCELONA MAPS:
Édigraphie
STREET MAPS:
Touring Club Italiano
PRODUCTION
Catherine Bourrabier

Translated by Matthew Clarke
and typeset by The Write Idea
in association with
First Edition Translations Ltd,
Cambridge, UK

Printed in Italy by
Editoriale Lloyd

Authors
VIENNA

Things you need to know and Where to shop:
Anne Laurent (1)
With responsibility for promoting Austrian
cinema worldwide on behalf of the
Austrian Film Commission, Anne Laurent is
a kind of roving cultural ambassadress for
her country. Her long experience of living
in Vienna, where she is always on the look-
out for interesting places, has allowed her
to uncover some of the capital's best-kept
secrets.

Where to stay and After dark:
Laurent Delage (2)
Laurent Delage, Vienna correspondent of
the French musical review *Classica*, is
fascinated by all aspects of the city's artistic
and cultural life. As well as acting as agent
for numerous artists, he possesses an in-
depth knowledge of the world of show
business. Also an indefatigable explorer of
Vienna's nightlife, Laurent takes particular
pleasure in sampling all the newest venues.

Where to eat:
Eva Bakos (3)
Eva Bakos is a writer whose output
includes guides to Vienna, Friuli, Venice and
southern Austria. Besides working on
movie scripts, she has already published
several novels – *Das gläserne Wappen, Villa
im Veneto, Sehnsucht nach Salina* – and a
history of Viennese cuisine. Her two
forthcoming books are *Wilde Wienerinnen*, a
story of unconventional Viennese society,
and a collection of recipes.

What to see and Further afield:
Karin Schiefer (4)
Karin Schiefer writes for several Austrian
dailies and periodicals on the cinema,
theater and literature. Having also
collaborated on several travel guides
covering the whole of Austria, she was an
obvious choice to edit the sightseeing
sections of our City Guide.

Contents

Things you need to know → 6

Where to stay → 16

Where to eat → 38

After dark → 64

What to see → 84

Further afield → 120

Where to shop → 128

Finding your way → 150

Key

- ☎ telephone number
- ➠ fax number
- ● price or price range
- ⊙ opening hours
- ▣ credit cards accepted
- ◪ credit cards not accepted
- ▼ toll-free number
- @ e-mail/website address
- ★ tips and recommendations

Access

- Ⓜ subway station(s)
- ▣ bus
- Ⓟ private parking
- ⅏ parking attendant
- ⬥ no facilities for the disabled
- ⬛ train
- ▣ car
- ⛴ boat

Hotels

- ☏ telephone in room
- ▥ fax in room on request
- ◩ minibar in room
- ▤ television in room
- ▥ air-conditioned rooms
- ⊙ 24-hour room service
- ▩ caretaker
- ⚹ babysitting
- ▦ meeting room(s)
- ⋈ no pets
- ♥ breakfast
- ☕ open for tea/coffee
- ♨ restaurant
- ♪ live music
- ◎ disco
- ✦ garden, patio or terrace
- ❀ gym, fitness club
- ≋ swimming pool, sauna

Restaurants

- ⬧ vegetarian food
- ✑ view
- ¶ formal dress required
- ⊿ smoking area
- ▼ bar

Museums and galleries

- ⊞ on-site store(s)
- ▤ guided tours
- ▣ café

Stores

- ⬥ branches, outlets

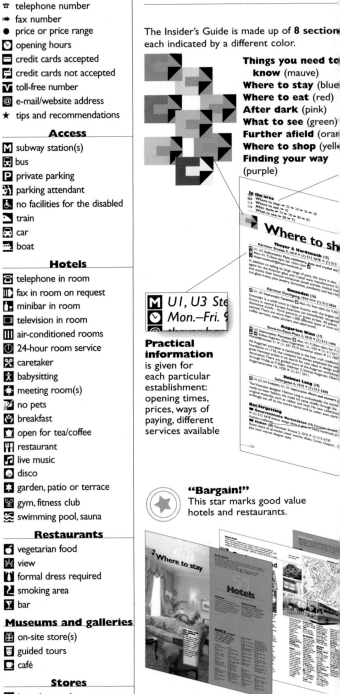

The Insider's Guide is made up of **8 section** each indicated by a different color.

Things you need to know (mauve)
Where to stay (blue)
Where to eat (red)
After dark (pink)
What to see (green)
Further afield (orar
Where to shop (yell
Finding your way (purple)

In the area
Where to stay: ➠ 22 — 24 — 26 — 28
Where to eat: ➠ 42
After dark: ➠ 74 — 78 — 80 — 82
What to see: ➠ 88 — 92

Where to sh

Theyer & Hardtmuth (15)
Ⓜ U1, U3 Stephansplatz, Paw... menswear, glass and crystal wa
⊙ Mon.–Fri. 9:30am-

Gmunden (16)
Ⓜ U1, U3 Stephansplatz Ceramic ⊙ Mon.–Fri. 9am–5pm; Sat. 9:30

Augarten Wien (17)
Ⓜ U1, U2, U4 Stock-im-Eisen-Platz 3, 1010 ☎ (1) 512 1494

Helmet Lang (18)
Ⓜ U1, U2, U4 Karlsplatz; U1, U2 Stephansplatz ● Seilergasse 6, 1010 ☎ (1) 512 2588

Not forgetting
Österreichische Werkstätten (19) Kärntner
☎ (1) 512 2418

Haban (20) Kärntner Straße 2, 1010 ☎ (1) 512 6730

Practical information
is given for each particular establishment: opening times, prices, ways of paying, different services available

Ⓜ U1, U3 Ste
⊙ Mon.–Fri. 9

"Bargain!"
This star marks good value hotels and restaurants.

Where to stay

Hotels

How to use this guide

In the area

- **Where to stay:** ➡ 22 ➡ 24 ➡
- **Where to eat:** ➡ 42
- **After dark:** ➡ 74 ➡ 78 ➡ 80 ➡
- **What to see:** ➡ 88 ➡ 92

The section **"In the area"** refers you (➡ 00) to other establishments that are covered in a different section of the guide but found in the same area of the city.

Kärntner Strasse/Stock-im-Eisen-Platz

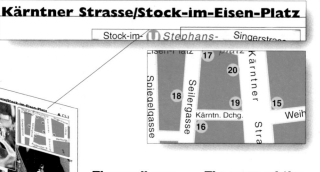

The small map shows all the establishments mentioned and others described elsewhere but found "in the area", by the color of the section.

The name of the district is given above the map. A grid reference (**A** B-C 2) enables you to find it in the section on Maps at the end of the book.

Not forgetting
■ **Österreichische Werkst…**

The section "Not forgetting" lists other useful addresses in the same area.

The opening page to each section contains an index ordered alphabetically (Getting there), by subject or by district (After dark) as well as useful addresses and advice.

The section "Things you need to know" covers information on getting

to Vienna and day-to-day life in the city.

Theme pages introduce a selection of establishments on a given topic.

The "Maps" section comprises: street index, plan of Vienna's subway system and 5 detailed maps.

The Orient Express
Vienna is thirteen hours from Paris by
train, so you will need to book sleeping-
car accommodation... But following in
Hercule Poirot's footsteps will set you
back around £200 or 320 US$.

Getting there

STANDARD

Cutting the cost of air travel

Round-trip tickets are the cheapest,
but must be booked in advance.
Travel agents and discount ticket
agencies will help you get the best
deal; prices vary between airlines
and according to times and dates
of flights. Ask about reductions for
weekend trips.

Calendar

Public holidays are: January 1 and 6, Easter Monday, May 1, Ascension Day, Whit Monday, Corpus Christi, August 15, October 26 (National Holiday), November 1, The Feast of the Immaculate Conception (December 8), Christmas Day and December 26. Vienna looks spectacularly beautiful in winter after a snowfall. One disadvantage of visiting the city in high summer is that some museums and galleries may be closed.

51 Things you need to Know

Getting Information

Austrian National Tourist Office: 30 St George St, London W1R 0AL 020 7629 0461
Austrian National Tourist Office: 500 Fifth Ave. Suite 2009–2022, New York, NY 10110. Tel: 212 944 6880; Fax: 212 730 4568 www.anto.com
You should also try logging on to the following Internet sites, which are full of useful facts and tips:
@ http://www.info.wien.at
@ http://www.magwien.gv.at
These allow you to download city maps pinpointing places of interest to tourists. You can also reserve hotel rooms and even seats at some shows.

Formalities

Citizens of European countries can enter Austria using an identity card or passport – valid up to five months after expiry date. On your return from vacation, you can reclaim the costs of any medical treatment; obtain form E111 from the health authority in your home country before traveling. This will be exchanged on the spot for a medical certificate (*Krankenschein*) at the Wiener Gebietskrankenkasse, *Wienerbergstrasse 15–19, 1010 Wien* (🔲 7A, 15A), Dept E64a
🕐 Mon.–Thu. 8am–2pm; Fri. 8am–1pm

INDEX

Flights from the UK: British Airways: Gatwick and Heathrow, daily.
Austrian Airlines: Heathrow, daily. Lauda Air: most days, Gatwick.
USA: there are direct or one-stop flights by Austrian Airlines, Delta and
Lauda – check with the airline for availability. Vienna's airport, Wien-

Getting there

Airport services (Wien-Schwechat)

Information
☽ 24hrs
☎ (1) 700 722331
➠ (1) 700 722333

Lost luggage
☎ (1) 700 762522

Police and Emergency Services
☎ (1) 700 7133

Lost property
Arrivals lounge
☽ 9am–5pm
☎ (1) 700 72197

Tourist information
Arrivals lounge
☽ 8.30am–9pm

Airlines
Austrian Airlines
Information and reservations
☎ (1) 700 71789
☽ *Mon.–Fri..
8am–6pm, Sat.,
Sun. and Bank
Holidays
8am–5pm*
(UK ☎ 020 7434
7300; US ☎ 800
843 0002)

British Airways
Information and reservations
☎ (1) 795 67567
(UK ☎ 0345
222111; US
☎ 800 247 9297)

Delta
Information and reservations
☎ (1) 512 6647
(UK ☎ 0800
414767; US ☎
800 241 4141)

Lauda Air
Information and reservations
☎ (1) 700 07733
(UK ☎ 020 7630
5549; US ☎ 800
588 8399)
*Note: Several
airlines have offices
in the city center.*

To the city center

Trains and buses
link the airport
with the main
railroad stations:
Wien-Mitte,
Wien-Nord,
Südbahnhof and
Westbahnhof.

Buses
A shuttle (journey
time: 30 mins)
operates between
the airport and

the City Air
Terminal at Wien
Mitte – in the
Hilton Hotel
☽ *6.30am–
11.30pm, every
20 mins; 11.30pm–
1am and 5.30–
6.30am, every
30 mins*
● *70 schillings
Allow 30 mins to
Südbahnhof and
45 mins to
Westbahnhof.*
☽ *7.10am–
11.10pm, every
hour, with additional
departures at
5.30am and
6.20am*
● *70 schillings*

Train
The station for the
high-speed S-Bahn,
which also serves

Schwechat, is 12 miles southeast of the city on the A4 freeway.

Wien Mitte, is beneath the arrivals lounge. Cheaper, but less comfortable, than the bus shuttle.
🕐 *Departures every 30 mins; journey time: 35 mins*
● *38 schillings*
Information
☎ *(1) 580 035398*
Taxis
The stand is opposite the exit of the arrivals lounge.
● *Allow at least*

400 schillings to the city center.
Information
☎ *(1) 700 735910*
➡ *(1) 700 732717*
Car rental
On the left as you leave the arrivals lounge.
Avis
☎ *(1) 700 732700*
Hertz
☎ *(1) 700 732661*
Sixt
☎ *(1) 700 73651*
Budget
☎ *(1) 700 73271*
Denzel Europcar
☎ *(1) 700 733316.*

Hotels

Sofitel
☎ *(1) 701510*
➡ *(1) 706 2828*
@*sofitel@atnet.at*
http://www.vienna-airport-hotels.at/wien
136 rooms, 6 suites, parking for 100 cars, with conference room, bar and restaurant.
Novotel
☎ *(1) 701070*
➡ *(1) 707 3239*

@*novotel@atnet.at*
http://www.novotel.at
183 rooms, parking for 80 cars, conference room, bar and restaurant.

Cafés

🕐 Open 24 hrs. in summer and 6am–midnight in winter (arrivals); 6am–10pm (departures).

Drivers using Austrian freeways must display a permit on their vehicles. This can be bought at the border, in post offices, at tobacconists', gas stations or from the ÖAMTC (Touring Club). For vehicles up to 3.5 t, reckon on 550 schillings for a year's permit, 150 schillings for 2 months,

Getting there

By train

Information in Vienna
☎ (1) 1717
🕐 daily, 24 hrs.
@ http://www.oebb.at

Reservations
☎ (1) 1700
🕐 daily
7am–10pm

Westbahnhof (1)
Terminus for trains arriving from France and Switzerland. Connections with subway system (U3 and U6) and streetcar service D.

Hotel bookings
🕐 6.15am–11pm

Lost property
Südbahnhof ☎ (1)

5800; from booths on station 35656; outside normal hours (1) 35658
🕐 Mon.–Fri. 7.30am–3.30pm

Südbahnhof (2)
Serves southern and eastern Europe, including Hungary.

Wien-Mitte (3) and Franz-Josefs-Bahnhof
Stations for the national network.

Wien-Mitte – the station for the airport – is also a bus terminus.

By car
If stopped by the police, motorists are expected to produce their driver's license and an international insurance certificate for the vehicle being driven. All vehicles must display international license plates – or the new European Union plates. It is illegal not to carry a first-aid box and a warning triangle.

Legal alcohol level
The maximum permitted level is 0.5 mg/l.

Speed limits
Freeways: 130 km/h or 81 mph. Country roads: 100 km/h or 62 mph. In town: 50km/h or 31mph.

Gasoline
Unleaded 98
● 11.40 schillings
Diesel
● 8.40 schillings

Breakdown assistance
ÖAMTC (Touring Club)
☎ (1) 120
ARBÖ
☎ (1) 123

Freeways
The Autobahnen

70 schillings for up to 10 days.

are signposted in white on a blue background. Except for certain stretches – usually in the mountains – they are toll-free.

Getting to Vienna

From Salzburg, the A1 (4) leads to Vienna via Linz and St Pölten. From Vienna, the A4 (6) continues to the airport and eventually toward Budapest (156 miles).

Tourist information

Look for information centers on entering Vienna: **A1, Wien-Auhof layby**

🕐 Apr.–Oct. 8am–10pm; Nov. 9am–7pm; Dec.–Mar. 10am–6pm
A2, Zentrum/ Triester Strasse exit
🕐 Apr.–May and Oct. 9am–7pm; July–Sep. 8am–10pm.

Driving

Public transport is first-class – an excellent reason not to use your car during your stay.

Parking lots

There are numerous underground parking lots. Prices are always displayed on-site.

Parking regulations

In the city center, parking is subject to time limits. In the restricted area (*Kurzparkzone*) the limit between 9am and 8pm is one and a half hours. You also need to buy a ticket (*Kurzparkscheine*), obtainable at a tobacconist's (*Tabak-Trafik*) or at stations.

● *6 schillings for 30 min*

However, hotels without garage facilities will offer clients a Parkkarte valid for the whole day. (*Parkkarte*).

● *50 schillings per day*

Warning!

Keep a look-out for streetcars, which always have priority, and passengers entering or alighting from them.

Arriving by boat

It is possible, provided you have the time, to get to Vienna by boat along the Danube. Board at Passau (railroad connection); the journey lasts one and a half days.
☎ (1) 58880
➡ (1) 588 80440
@ http://www.ddsg-blue-danube.at

Vienna boasts a reliable public transport system serving virtually all areas and, compared with many capitals, is not overburdened with traffic. Within the Ring there are also numerous pedestrianized streets — outlined in red on the mini-maps — ideal for a relaxed stroll and sampling

➡ Getting around

Public transport

Information
☎ (1) 790 9105
🕐 5.30am–10pm;
Sat., Sun. and
public holidays
8.30am–5pm
@ post@
wienerlinien.co.at

Subway
The subway system was only built in the 1970s. There are 5 lines (U1, U2, U3, U4, U6 ➡ 164), the stations are signposted with a white **U** on a blue background.

Schnellbahn
The S-Bahn is the high-speed train linking the city center with the suburbs. Its logo is a white **S** – in the form of a lightning-flash – in a blue circle.

Buses and streetcars
To get away from the city center, use the buses or streetcars. The latter offer a pleasant way of exploring the capital.
🕐 5–0.30am
● Children under 6 travel free; 6–15, free Sun., public holidays and when schools closed
A one-way ticket gives access to all destinations – by any means of transport – for one continuous journey.
● 17 schillings (11 schillings for children over 6)

If you have change, you can use the automatic ticket machines on the buses and streetcars. Note: drivers do not sell tickets.
● 22 schillings if tickets bought on board
There is also a night-time bus service.
🕐 0.30–4am.
● 15 schillings. You can make savings by purchasing season tickets. (Identity photograph required.)
● 155 schillings Monthly
● 60 schillings 24 hours
● 150 schillings 72 hours
The Umwelt-Streifennetzkarte is

a booklet of eight coupons. Once validated, each allows one person to travel free all day.
● 265 schillings
The advantage of this scheme, beside the saving in cost, is its flexibility for family travel, as the coupons are not restricted to named individuals.

The Wien Kart
● 210 schillings
This allows unrestricted travel over the entire bus, streetcar and subway network for a period of 72 hours. Also, it gives the purchaser the right to a reduction of 20–50% in the cost of entry to the principal

the many cafés
and stores.

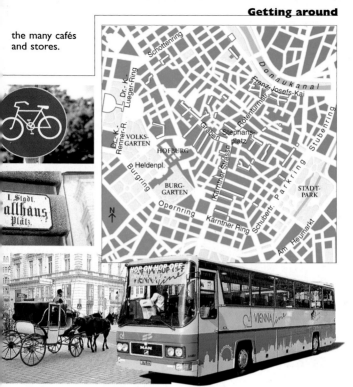

tourist attractions
and 10–15% off
purchases in
certain cafés and
stores. The Wien-
Kart can be
bought at
tobacconists',
tourist
information
centers and
selected hotels.

**Lost property
(public
transport)**
☎ (1) 7909105

Taxis

There are plenty
of taxi stands in
Vienna: at
stations, outside
the main hotels,
on the Ring, and
in the vicinity of
major tourist
attractions. There
is a surcharge on
fares between
11pm and 6am,
on Sundays and
on public
holidays.

Radio-taxis
☎ 31300 ☎ 40100
☎ 60160 ☎ 81400
Tips
Round up your
fare to the next
5 or 10 shillings.

By bicycle

Vienna has a huge
network of bicycle
lanes which let
you negotiate the
city streets in
safety; one runs
alongside the Ring,
another leads to
the Prater.
Information
Argus publish a
themed map for
devotees of pedal
power: the
*Stadtplan Wien
für RadfahrerInnen.*
☎ (1) 505 8435
➡ (1) 505 090719
@ service@
argus.or.at
Frankenberggasse
11 - 1040 Wien
● 118 shillings
Tours
Bicycle rental

companies
organize tours to
explore the city,
inc. group tours:
Vienna Bike
☎ (1) 319 1258
Pedal Power
☎ (1) 729 7234
**Radverleih
Salztorbrücke**
☎ (1) 535 3422

Guided
Tours

**Vienna Guide
Service**
☎ (1) 440 30940
➡ (1) 440 2825
On foot
☎ (1) 895363
Themed
itineraries:
Jugendstil, the cafés
of Vienna, etc.
By Pullman
*Vienna
Sightseeing Tours*
☎ (1) 712 46830
Cityrama
☎ (1) 534130
By streetcar
☎ (1) 790 944026
From May to the
beginning of

October, the
public transport
authorities run
sightseeing tours
of the city using
old-fashioned
streetcars.
By boat
*DDSG Blue
Danube*
May–Oct.
☎ (1) 588800
➡ (1) 588 80440
Sightseeing trip
through Vienna
along the Danube:
● 180 shillings
One-day round
trip to Budapest:
● 1,100 shillings
**Horse-drawn
carriages**
On the
Stephansplatz,
Heldenplatz and
around the
Staatsoper.

The numerous brochures published in all languages by the Tourist Information Office contain information on everyday life and the attractions on offer. In particular, there is a free mini-plan of the city. Finally, if a problem does occur, you can always count on the natural

Getting by

Money

Coins and bills

The unit of currency is the Austrian schilling (ÖS or ATS), subdivided into 100 groschen. Coins in circulation are 2, 5, 10 and 50 groschen, plus 1, 5, 10 and 20 ÖS. Denominations of bills are 20, 50, 100, 500, 1000 and 5000 ÖS.

Exchange rate

$1 is roughly 13 schillings. At the time of writing, 21.26 Austrian schillings were worth £1 sterling or 1.58 US$. The easiest way to obtain currency is to use the automatic bill dispensers at various banks. You can also change money in the larger hotels, at the airport, and in post offices.

Credit cards

The custom of paying in cash is still very much part of the Austrian way of life, and some establishments may not accept credit cards. Best to ask before you make a purchase… or sit down at table!

Media

Local press

The country's leading daily papers are *Die Presse, Der Standard* and *Kurier*. One of the 'popular' dailies is *Kronen Zeitung*. *Falter* (weekly) gives essential information on the city's cultural activities, while *Wien Magazin* – published in four languages – is a monthly aimed at foreign visitors.

Foreign press

Papers can be bought from news-stands in the city center. A wide selection of foreign newspapers is also on sale at stands in stations.

Radio

In April 1998 Austria's 'Free Radios' were born. There are four public radio stations, including Blue Danube Radio which broadcasts programs in English and French.

Television

There are two public channels (ORF1 and ORF2). Most hotels can receive broadcasts in several languages via cable and satellite.

Telephones

Country/area codes

To call Vienna from another town in Austria, dial 02 22 followed by the number required. From abroad, dial 0043 followed by 1, then the subscriber's number. To call another country from Vienna, dial 00, then the country code (USA: 1, UK: 44), the city/area code (minus initial 0) and then the subscriber's number.

kindness and
helpfulness of
the Viennese.

Tolls

There are
reduced tariffs for
phone calls before
8am, after 6pm,
and on public
holidays. Note:
calls made from
hotels carry a
high surcharge.

Mobile phones

Austria is well
covered by
agreements
between
European mobile
phone operators.
But be aware that
heavy surcharges
bring the cost of
calls to over 50p
(80¢) per minute!

Telephone booths

Booths are gray
with a yellow
band at the top.
To make a call,
you need change
or a phone card
(48 or 95
schillings)
obtainable at a
tobacconist's.

Postal Services (1)

To UK:
● 6 schillings for
airmail postcards.
● 7 schillings for
airmail letters.
To USA:
● 8.5 schillings for
airmail postcards.
● 14.5 schillings
for airmail letters.
◷ Mon.–Fri.
8am–noon and
2–6pm
Post offices in
stations and the
Central Post
Office
(Fleischmarkt 19)
are open daily.
◷ 24 hrs.
Automatic stamp
dispensers are
installed outside
main post offices.
You can also buy
stamps from
news-stands.
Telegram service
☎ 190

Tourist Information Offices (2)

Information

Kärntner Strasse
38
◷ 9am–7pm
Ⓜ U1, U2, U4
Karlsplatz
Information by mail
Wiener
Tourismusverband
A-1025 Wien
Information by telephone
☎ (1) 211140
➟ (1) 216 8492
Information by e-mail and Internet
@ inquiries@
info.wien.at
http://info.wien.at
Information for young visitors (Jugend Info-Wien) (3)
Dr.-Karl-Renner-
Ring/Bellaria
Passage
Ⓜ U2, U3
Volkstheater
☎ (1) 1799
@ Jugendinfo.vie
@blackbox.ping.at
◷ Mon.–Fri.

noon–7pm; Sat.,
Sun. and school
holidays
10am–7pm

Lost Property

Fundamt
Wasagasse 22,
1090 Wien
☎ (1) 313440
◷ Mon.–Fri.
8am–noon
Ⓜ U2 Schottentor-
Universität

Emergency Services

Pharmacies
(Apotheke) are
usually
recognizable by
a red letter **A**.
Police
☎ (1) 133
Ambulance
☎ (1) 144
Emergency doctors
☎ (1) 141
Duty pharmacists
☎ (1) 1550

Where to stay

The man with the golden keys

Do you need tickets for the theater or the concert? Want to dine out in a typical restaurant or need information about the city… ? The hotel concierge has all the answers. Don't hesitate to call on his services!

Book ahead!

It is essential to reserve your hotel accommodation well in advance in the high season (Apr. 1–Oct. 31). In the low season (Nov. 1–Mar. 31), most hotels offer reduced tariffs.
Wien-Hotels: Reservation Center of the Vienna Tourist Office
☎ (1) 211 14444 ➡ (1) 211 14445 @ rooms@info.wien.at

51 Hotels

THE INSIDER'S FAVORITES

Pensions

Obviously, these do not have restaurants or conference facilities – but the rooms are always pleasant and welcoming. With luck you may get breakfast too. Some pensions have rooms with self-catering facilities.

Youth Hostels

Myrtengasse 7, 1070 Wien, and Neustiftgasse 85, 1070 Wien, ☎ (1) 523 6316 ➡ (1) 523 5849 Total of 240 beds at the two addresses. Advance booking recommended.

◢ **Where to stay**

Hotel Sacher (1)
Philharmonikerstrasse 4, 1010 ☎ (1) 514560 ➡ (1) 514 56810

Ⓜ *Karlsplatz/Oper* ▣ *Karlsplatz/Oper* ▧ *108 rooms* ●●●●● *27 suites* ▱ Ⓞ
▣ ▣ ⅢⅬ Ⅼ Ⅲ ⑪ *Sacher* ⓨ ▣ ▣ ▨ ▨ ▣ @ *hotel@sacher.com*
http://www.sacher.com.

The hotel was founded in 1876 by Eduard Sacher, the son of the Franz
Sacher who created the famous *Sachertorte* in 1840. Things have never
looked back since, with 270,000 gateaux produced every year. You can
try one on the spot at the Café Sacher or take some away as souvenirs
of your self-indulgence, though there is a worldwide delivery service.
This is one of the city's most luxurious establishments. However, despite
all its historical associations, what really makes the Sacher is its unique
Viennese atmosphere.

Hotel Bristol (2)
Kärntner Ring 1, 1010 ☎ (1) 515 16536/537 ➡ (1) 515 16550

Ⓜ *Karlsplatz/Oper* Ⓟ ▧ *131 rooms* ●●●●● *11 suites* ▱ Ⓞ ▣ ▣ ⅢⅬ Ⅼ
Ⅲ ⑪ *Korso, Sirk* ⓨ ▨ ▣ ▣ ▨ ▦ ⎞ @ *Hotel_Bristol@sheraton.com*
http://www.luxurycollection.com/Bristol

Though recently enlarged and refurbished, this hotel – dating from 1892 –
preserves the discreet charm so much appreciated by the aristocracy of
the late 19th century. All modern comforts and conveniences blend
effortlessly with its historical heritage, which includes works of art and fine
period furniture. The front rooms have a grandstand view of the Staatsoper
just across the square. However, you may wish to exchange the
contemplation of this temple of operatic art for the peace and quiet of
apartments overlooking the Mahlerstrasse. A whole floor, including meeting
room and office accommodation, is set aside for business travelers.

Astoria (3)
Kärntner Strasse 32-34, 1010 ☎ (1) 515770 ➡ (1) 515 7782

Ⓜ *U2, U4 Karlsplatz/Oper 108 rooms* ●●● ▱ ▣ ▣ Ⅼ ⑪ ⓨ ▣ ▣
@ *astoria@atnet.at*

You will probably love the spacious rooms and traditional atmosphere of
the Astoria, built in 1912. Excellent soundproofing ensures you won't be
disturbed, even in the rooms overlooking the busy pedestrianized zone
of the Kärntner Strasse.

Zur Wiener Staatsoper (4)
Krugerstrasse 11, 1010 ☎ (1) 513 1274 ➡ (1) 513 177415

Ⓜ *U2, U4 Karlsplatz/Oper 22 rooms* ●● ▱ ▣ ▣
@ *office@zurwienerstaatsoper.at, http://www.zurwienerstaatsoper.at*

As its name indicates, this family establishment is only a step or two
away from the Opera. The rooms are clean and well maintained, with
nice individual touches.

Not forgetting

■ **Opernring Hotel (5)** Opernring 11, 1010 ☎ (1) 587 5518
➡ (1) 587 551829 ●●●. ■ **Pension Suzanne (6)** Walfischgasse 4, 1010
☎ (1) 513 2507 ➡ (1) 513 2500 ●●

2

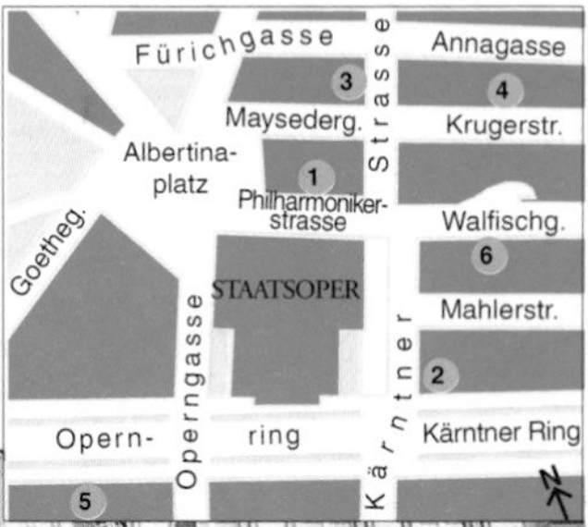
Fürichgasse
Annagasse
3
4
Maysederg.
Krugerstr.
Albertina-
platz
1
Philharmoniker-
strasse
Walfischg.
6
Goetheg.
STAATSOPER
Mahlerstr.
2
Opern-
ring
Kärntner Ring
Operngasse
Kärntner Strasse
5

HOTEL SACHER
Sacher
Sacher
1

HOTEL ASTORIA

Staatsoper
4

3 Palatial hotel or family establishment? Plenty of choice around the Staatsoper!

6

5

➤ Where to stay

Ana Grand Hotel (7)
Kärntner Ring 9, 1010 ☎ (1) 515800 ➡ (1) 515 1313

Ⓜ *Karlsplatz/Oper* 🚇 *Karlsplatz/Oper* 🅿 🛏 *205 rooms* ●●●●● *30 suites* ▭
⊙ ▣ 🕾 Ⅲ 🛗 Ⅲ 🍴 *Grand Café, Le Ciel, Unkai,* 🍽 ▢ ⚙ ✗ ♿ ✚ ✗ @
sales@anagrand.com, http://www.anagrand.com

The former Grand Hotel reopened its doors in 1994 after a four-year facelift, and now offers some of Vienna's most luxurious accommodation. Many famous names in the musical world – from Mstislav Rostropovich to Luciano Pavarotti, not forgetting U2 – have used this hotel as their base. Its rooms, as well as being very comfortable, enjoy particularly good soundproofing, which is something worth considering when you are staying in a city center. Shopaholics note: there is direct access from the hotel to the Ringstrassen Galerien, a new shopping mall.

Imperial (8)
Kärntner Ring 16, 1010 ☎ (1) 501 10333/423 ➡ (1) 501 10440

Ⓜ *Karlsplatz/Oper* 🅿 🛏 *96 rooms* ●●●●● *32 suites* ▭ ⊙ ▣ 🕾 Ⅲ 🛗
Ⅲ 🍴 *Imperial* 🍽 ▢ ⚙ ♿ ✚ ✗ ▦ @ *Hotel_Imperial@sheraton.com*
http://www.luxurycollection.com/Imperial

This establishment occupies a former royal palace. The building was, in fact, built for Prince Philip of Würtemberg, who presented it to his bride as a wedding gift. Some time later, major urban redevelopment – connected with the construction of the Ring – threatened to break up the palace park, so the prince decided to sell the property. The palace was transformed into a hotel, opened in 1873 by Franz-Joseph in person. A major-domo meets each visitor on arrival, presenting a personalized visiting card with the temporary address, explaining all the facilities and answering any questions. He then remains at the visitor's disposal twenty-four hours a day. Charlie Chaplin, one of the Imperial's megastar clients, considered the accommodation here to be the best he had ever seen. You can hardly disagree; the furnishings of these vast rooms are just as opulent as the architecture. Moreover, in 1994 the Imperial was voted one of the best hotels in the world – and this is where visiting ministers and Heads of State are lodged. Many internationally known musicians also stay here; the hotel is just opposite the Musikverein, so they only need pop out the back to reach the performers' entrance.

Am Schubertring (9)
Schubertring 11, 1010 ☎ (1) 717020 ➡ (1) 713 9966

Ⓜ *Stadtpark* 🚇 *Schwarzenbergplatz* 🅿 *approximately* **39 rooms** ●●●
3 suites ▭ ▣ 🕾 🛗 Ⅲ 🍽 ✗ ✚ @ *aschu@atnet.at*

This delightful little hotel, within a stone's throw of the Konzerthaus and the Muzikverein, was opened in 1984. It occupies a handsome late 19th-century building between the Schwarzenberg Platz and the Stadtpark. The rooms, many of them converted attics, are quiet, with attractive Biedermeier or Jugendstil furnishings but also all modern facilities. Another star feature is the service; you will have trouble finding anything to grumble about!

7 The Ana Grand Hotel dates from 1870: the time of the construction of the Ring, the peripheral boulevard which encircles the historic heart of Vienna.

◢ Where to stay

Ambassador (10)
Kärntner Strasse 22, 1010 ☎ (1) 51466 ➠ (1) 513 2999

Ⓜ *Karlsplatz/Oper* Ⓟ *105 rooms* ●●●● *21 suites* 🔲 🔘 🔲 🔲 🔲 🔲 🔲
🔲 *Lehar* 🔲 🔲 🔲 🔲 @ *office@ambassador.at, http://www.ambassador.at*

Situated halfway between the Staatsoper and the Stephansdom, in the
elegant traffic-free zone of the Kärtner Strasse, this establishment has
been offering top-quality service for over a century. The surroundings
are welcoming and impeccably maintained; the furnishings of the big, airy
rooms show the same attachment to tradition.

Mailbergerhof (11)
Annagasse 7, 1010 ☎ (1) 512 06410 ➠ (1) 512 064110

Ⓜ *Karlsplatz/Oper* Ⓟ *40 rooms* ●●● *6 apartments* 🔲 🔲 🔲 🔲 🔲 🔲 🔲 🔲

In a nutshell, peaceful and very well situated. The hotel is in a tranquil
street very near the Kärtner Strasse, the heart of the traffic-free zone.
This means it is also only a brief walk from the Staatsoper, the
Stadtpark, the Ronacher Theater and the prestigious Verein concert hall.
However, the Mailbergerhof has other cards to play: it has offered a
friendly welcome ever since its opening in 1976, and occupies a Baroque
building listed as a national monument.

Römischer Kaiser (12)
Annagasse 16, 1010 ☎ (1) 512 7751 ➠ (1) 512 775113

Ⓜ *U2, U4 Karlsplatz/Oper* *24 rooms* ●●● 🔲 🔲 🔲 🔲 🔲 🔲 🔲 @
info@rkhotel.bestwestern.at

Constructed in 1684 by the Court Chancellor Johann Hüber, the
building is in Baroque style; in the time of Maria Theresa it housed the
polytechnic school. Since 1904, it has been run with every attention to
detail by the same family, who unfailingly provide clients with
accommodation that is both tasteful and comfortable.

Pension Aviano (13)
Marco-D'Aviano-Gasse 1, 1010 ☎ (1) 512 8330 ➠ (1) 512 8330/6

Ⓜ *Karlsplatz/Oper* *17 rooms* ●● 🔲 🔲 🔲

A pension with very reasonable prices considering its city-center
position, occupying the top story of a late 19th-century block. All rooms
are equipped with satellite TV; several have cooking facilities.

Europa (14)
Kärntner Strasse 18, 1010 ☎ (1) 515940 ➠ (1) 513 8138

Ⓜ *Karlsplatz/Oper* *113 rooms* ●●● 🔲 🔲 🔲 🔲 🔲 🔲 🔲 🔲 🔲 🔲 @
europa.wien@austria-trend.at, http://www.austria-trend.at

The Europa dates from the 1950s, but underwent a complete renovation
in 1998. New rooms have been added on the first floor, while the
existing ones have enjoyed a makeover. All now have air-conditioning.
The Martini bar is a favorite haunt of TV and radio personalities.

Historic facades conceal numerous hotels in the traffic-free zone of the Kärntner Strasse.

In the area
➦ **Where to eat:** ➥ 40 ➥ 42 ➥ 44
➦ **After dark:** ➥ 70 ➥ 74 ➥ 78 ➥ 80 ➥ 82
➦ **What to see:** ➥ 88
➦ **Where to shop:** ➥ 136 ➥ 140 ➥ 142

➤ Where to stay

Hotel Royal (15)
Singerstrasse 3, 1010 ☎ (1) 515680 ➥ (1) 513 9698

Ⓜ *Stephansplatz* **77 rooms** ●●● *4 apartments* ▢ ▣ ☎ ⌘ ⊞ *Firenze Enoteca* Ⓨ ✪ ⛷

A pilgrims' inn (*Zum Roten Apfl*) stood on this spot three hundred years ago… but as with many city-center buildings, this was badly damaged by air-raids during World War II. After reconstruction was completed in 1960, it became the Hotel Royal. Its terrace overlooks the old city and the superb glazed tile roof of the Stephansdom. The ground-floor restaurant is frequented by opera stars; its name – Firenze Enoteca – is in no way pretentious: it boasts the finest wine cellar in the whole of Austria.

Kaiserin Elisabeth (16)
Weihburggasse 3, 1010 ☎ (1) 51526 ➥ (1) 51526-7

Ⓜ *Stephansplatz* **64 rooms** ●●● *3 suites* ▢ ▣ ☎ ⌘ Ⓨ ※
@ *kaiserin@ins.at*

This address in the heart of the old city has a proven history. In particular, it seems that Mozart lodged here in 1767, in a house later destroyed by Napoleon's troops. Rebuilt on a grander scale in 1809, the hotel was granted permission in 1910 to call itself the Kaiserin Elisabeth in homage to the Empress of Austria better known as Sissi. It still maintains its typically Viennese atmosphere, its warm welcome and its impeccable service.

Am Stephansplatz (17)
Stephansplatz 9, 1010 ☎ (1) 53405-0 ➥ (1) 53405-710/711

Ⓜ *Stephansplatz* ℙ **60 rooms** ●●● ▢ ▣ ☎ ⌘ Ⓨ ▢ ※
@ *hotel@stephansplatz.co.at, http://www.nethotels.com/amstephansplatz*

The hotel has the advantage of being very centrally located. It is in a mainly pedestrian zone with few on-street parking facilities, but this is no real drawback, as the hotel has its own parking lot. The rooms are furnished in a very warm, traditional style, offering exceptional views of the Stephansdom – you can admire the west front at your leisure – or watch the bustling activities in the Stephansplatz.

Pension City (18)
Bauermarkt 10, 1010 ☎ (1) 533 9521 ➥ (1) 535 5216

Ⓜ *U1,U3 Stephansplatz* **19 rooms** ● ▢ ▣ ☎ ⌘

This is to be found on the mezzanine floor. Don't be surprised by the bust and the plaque by the entrance. These are to commemorate the great Austrian poet and dramatist Franz Grillparzer, born here in 1791. Ideally located in a tranquil street close to the cathedral, this pension offers agreeable, recently renovated rooms at more than reasonable prices. Nineteenth-century and modern furniture happily rub shoulders, and the welcome is warm and hospitable.

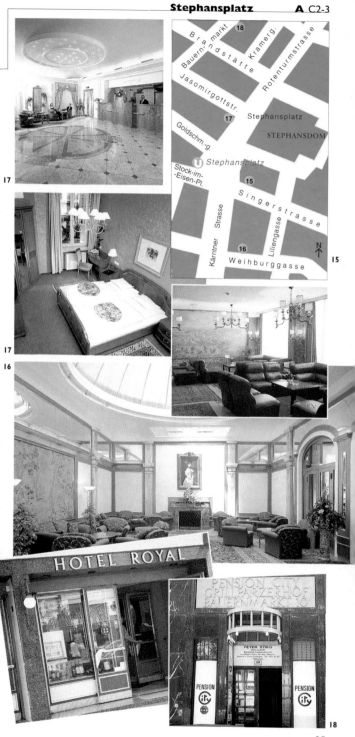

Brandmarkt
Bauernmarkt
Kramerg.
Rotenturmstrasse
Jasomirgottstr.
Stephansplatz
Goldschm.g.
STEPHANSDOM
Stephansplatz
Stock-im-Eisen-Pl.
Singerstrasse
Kärntner Strasse
Liliengasse
Weihburggasse

HOTEL ROYAL

PENSION CITY
GRILL PARZERHOF
BAUERNMARKT 10

▶ Where to stay

Graben Hotel (19)
Dorotheergasse 3, 1010 ☎ (1) 512 1531-0 ➡ (1) 512 1531-20

M *Stephansplatz* **46 rooms** ●●● ▭ ▣ ▣ ▐▌ ▥ *Altenberg, Trattoria Santo Stefano* @ *graben@kremslehner.hotels.or.at, http://www.kremslehner.hotels.or.at/graben*

The Graben was already in existence at the end of the 18th century under the name of *Zum Goldenen Jägerhorn*, one of its most frequent guests being the poet Franz Grillparzer. In the years immediately preceding World War I, it became a favorite meeting-place for literary figures such as Peter Altenberg, Franz Kafka and Max Brod. This period is recalled today by the Jugendstil furniture surviving in many of the rooms.

Hotel Wandl (20)
Petersplatz 9, 1010 ☎ (1) 53455-0 ➡ (1) 53455-77

M *Stephansplatz* **138 rooms** ●● ▭ ▣ ▣ @ *reservation@hotel-wandl.com http://www.nethotels.com/wandl*

The Wandl has been run for several generations by the same family and is admirably located for cultural visits and shopping. It is tucked away, in fact, behind the beautiful Baroque Church of St Peter – a short stroll from the Graben shopping mall, and not far either from the Michaelerplatz, where you will find the entrance to the Hofburg (Imperial Palace).

Hotel Amadeus (21)
Wildpretmarkt 5, 1010 ☎ (1) 533 8738 ➡ (1) 533 8738-38

M *Stephansplatz* **30 rooms** ●● ▭ ▣ ▣ ▐▌.

Numerous composers – particularly Johannes Brahms and Franz Schubert – frequented the inn known as *Zum Roten Igel* which stood on this site in the 19th century. The present owners have elected to pay homage to one of the 18th-century giants of music: Wolfgang Amadeus Mozart. Its clientele is a mixed bag: artists and students, but also business people. The original Biedermeier furnishings are still in existence.

Pension Nossek (22)
Graben 17, 1010 ☎ (1) 533 7041-0 ➡ (1) 535 3646

M *Stephansplatz* **26 rooms** ●● ▣ ▣

This pension enjoys a central position, and is synonymous with a warm welcome, agreeable, well maintained surroundings and reasonable prices. The Viennese will inform you that reception is on the first floor. Don't believe it! What they mean is, the floor above the Hochparterre and the mezzanine: in other words, the third floor!

Pension Pertschy im Palais Cavriani (23)
Habsburgergasse 5, 1010 ☎ (1) 534490 ➡ (1) 534 4949

M *U3 Herrengasse* **47 rooms** ●● ▭ ▣ ▣ ▐▌ ♿

Another useful address for anyone looking for a moderately priced room in the city center. You will find it between the Hofburg and the Graben, in an ocher-colored courtyard looking like a little piece of the Mediterranean transported to the heart of Vienna. A peaceful situation, with a convivial welcome and spacious rooms.

Parserg.

Kurrentg.

Kleeblattgasse

Tuchlauben

Wildpretmarkt

21

Brandstätte

Steindlg.

20

Bognerg.

Seitzerg.

Peters-

Naglerg.

platz

Goldschm.-g.

Kohlmarkt

Graben

22

Habsburgergasse

23

Bräunerstrasse

Dorotheerg.

19

Spiegelg.

20

21

22

23

19

In the area
▶ Where to eat: ➡ 40 ➡ 42
▶ After dark: ➡ 70, 78 ➡ 80
▶ What to see: ➡ 86 ➡ 88
▶ Where to shop: ➡ 136 ➡ 140

▶ Where to stay

König von Hungarn (24)
Schulerstrasse 10, 1010 ☎ (1) 51584-0 ➡ (1) 515848

Ⓜ *Stephansplatz* Ⓟ *approximately* **33 rooms** ●●● ▣ ▣ 🖼 📶 Ⅲ 🎴 ⓨ
✚ ✕

Since its establishment in 1815, this refined hotel has made it a point of
honor to offer a perfect welcome and perfect service. Situated near the
cathedral and the house where Mozart wrote *The Marriage of Figaro*, its
rooms are quiet, recently renovated and equipped with every comfort,
while the bright and colorful corridors are hung with hunting trophies.
There is an excellent restaurant and a well designed terrace with a bar.

Appartment-Pension Riemergasse (25)
Riemergasse 8, 1010 ☎ (1) 512 72200 ➡ (1) 513 7778

Ⓜ *Stubentor* Ⓟ **20 apartments** ●● 🖼 ▣ 🖼

This building, clearly dating from the early 1900s, contains a range of
accommodation from studio size to a big 270-sq ft apartment. The
rooms are quiet and practical. All have a kitchenette and the usual hotel
facilities and services, such as telephone, cable TV, daily cleaning.

Radisson SAS Palais Hotel (26)
Parkring 16, 1010 ☎ (1) 51517-0 ➡ 512 2216

Ⓜ *Stadtpark* Ⓟ 🏵 **246 rooms** ●●●●● *52 suites* ▣ ⓞ ▣ 🖼 Ⅱ▶ 📶 Ⅲ
🎴 *Le Siècle* ⓨ ▣ 🏵 🍴 ✚ 🎿 ⊞ @ *sales@viezh.rdsas.com*
http://www.radisson.com/vienna.at

The hotel occupies two splendid late 19th-century buildings fastidiously
restored between 1991 and 1994: the Palais Henckel von Donnersmarck
and the Palais Leitenberg. Catering primarily for business travelers, the
Radisson strives to combine the class of the big Ringstrasse hotels –
irreproachable service, for instance – with the comfort of more modern
establishments. One entire floor is devoted to business facilities, with
conference and meeting rooms. A fitness club and a good fish restaurant,
Le Siècle, will offer a pleasant break from work.

Vienna Marriott (27)
Parkring 12a, 1010 ☎ (1) 51518-0 ➡ (1) 515 18-6736

Ⓜ *U4 Stadtpark* Ⓟ **313 rooms** ●●●● *28 suites* 🎿 ▣ ⓞ ▣ 🖼 Ⅱ▶ 📶 Ⅲ
🎴 *Parkring Restaurant* ⓨ ▣ 🏵 🍴 ⊞ 🎿 ✚ 🎿 🎿 ⊞

The Vienna Marriott is situated opposite the Stadtpark on the Ring, and its
standards match up to what you would expect from a hotel chain with an
international reputation. Restaurant, café, three bars, swimming pool and
fitness center; also conference and seminar rooms, and other meeting
areas, with overall business facilities for 750 persons.

Not forgetting
■ Pension Domizil (28) Schulerstrasse 14, 1010 ☎ (1) 513 3199-0
➡ (1) 512 3484 ●●

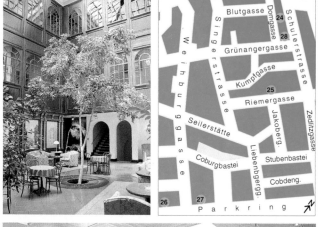

24

7

26

After a recent refurbishment, the Radisson now offers both the comfort and convenience of a modern hotel and century-old traditions.

28

26

In the area
■ ➔ Where to eat: ➔ 44 ➔ 48
■ ➔ After dark: ➔ 66 ➔ 68 ➔ 72 ➔ 74
■ ➔ What to see: ➔ 90 ➔ 94
■ ➔ Where to shop: ➔ 140 ➔ 148–149

▶Where to stay

Austria (29)
Am Fleischmarkt 20, 1010 ☎ (1) 51323 ➔ (1) 51523-506

Ⓜ *Schwedenplatz* 🅿 **42 rooms** ●● *4 apartments* ▤ ▣ 📺 🛗
@ *hotelaus@eunet.at, http://www.ping.at/members/hotelaus/*

Standing in a side street near the Donaukanal, this is a hotel for absolute peace and quiet. It is also a good place for lovers of chamber music as the Wiener Kammeroper is in the immediate vicinity. The surroundings are elegant and typically Viennese late 19th- and early 20th-century.

Kärntnerhof (30)
Grashofgasse 4, 1011 ☎ (1) 512 1923 ➔ (1) 513 222833

Ⓜ *Schwedenplatz* **43 rooms** ●● *3 apartments* ▣ 📺 ✂
@ *karntnerhof@netway.at, http://www.kartnerhof.com*

This very old establishment near the cathedral has won a loyal clientele, mainly by the warmth of its welcome. The Kärntnerhof is hidden away in a sleepy little street, just beside the Heiligenkreuzerhof. Go through the courtyard of the latter to find the Schönlaterngasse, a medieval lane steeped in legend.

Hotel Capricorno (31)
Am Schwedenplatz 3-4, 1010 ☎ (1) 533 3104-0 ➔ (1) 533 76714

Ⓜ *Schwedenplatz* 🅿 **46 rooms** ●● ▤ ▣ 📺 🛗 Ⅲ ✂
@ *capricorno@schick-hotels.com, http://www.schick-hotels.com*

From the balcony of one of the front rooms you should be able to see across the Donaukanal to the giant ferris wheel on the Prater. This is the room where Carol Reed shot one of the most memorable scenes in his movie *The Third Man*. From the lively Schwedenplatz it is only two subway stations to the Prater. This huge amusement park is one of the world's oldest and beloved of the Viennese.

Starlight Suiten Hotel (32)
Am Salzgries 12, 1010 ☎ (1) 533 9222 ➔ (1) 533 9222-11

Ⓜ *U1, U4 Schwedenplatz* 🅿 **49 suites** ●●● ▤ ▣ 📺 🛗 Ⅲ ✐ ✂
@ *reservations@starlighthotel.co.at, http://www.starlighthotel.co.at* ♨ *Starlight Suiten in der Renngasse 13, 1010 ☎ (1) 533 9989 ➔ (1) 533 9989-11 Starlightsuite am Heumarkt 15, 1030 ☎ (1) 535 9222 ➔ (1) 535 9222-11*

For the price of a single room in the same category of hotel, the Starlight offers en-suite accommodation: bedroom, bathroom and spacious living room with a work area. Modern, comfortable surroundings; even the minibar and the microwave have not been forgotten. Clients also have access to a sauna and a fitness center.

Not forgetting
■ **Schweizerhof** (33) Bauermarkt 22, 1010 ☎ (1) 533 1931
➔ (1) 533 0214 ▤ ▣ 📺 @ office@schweizerhof.at
http://www.schweizerhof.at ■ **Hotel Mercure Wien Zentrum**
(34) Fleischmarkt 1a, 1010 Vienne ☎ (1) 534600 ➔ (1) 534 60232 ●●●

◤ Where to stay

Hotel im Palais Schwarzenberg (35)
Schwarzenbergplatz 9, 1030 ☎ (1) 798 4515 ➡ (1) 798 4714

🗺 4A, 71, D 🅿 free 🛏 44 rooms ●●●●● 8 suites ▭ ◉ ▣ ☎ ▥ 🛗 ▥
🍽 Terrassen-Restaurant ▼ ✵ ✕ ✚ ✚ @ palais@schwarzenberg.via.at
http://www.relaischateaux.fr/schwarzenberg

In the 1960s, the former aristocratic residence of the Schwarzenbergs since 1727 was transformed into a hotel. An impressive building, owing its origins to two of Vienna's most talented architects: Lukas von Hildebrandt and Fischer von Erlach. There is a whole range of public rooms decorated with trompe l'oeil frescos and bedrooms with stately old furniture – and it has two original paintings by Reubens. A terrace restaurant overlooks a magnificent park which stretches away to meet the Belvedere Gardens. There are also tennis courts. Is this Vienna's most desirable address?

Hilton Vienna (36)
Am Stadtpark 1030 ☎ (1) 71700-0 ➡ (1) 712 8012

Ⓜ Wienmitte 600 rooms ●●●● 50 suites ▭ ◉ ▣ ☎ ▥ 🛗 ▥ 🍽
Brasserie Arcadia, Sam's ▼ ▯ ✵ ✕ ✚ ✵ ⊞ @ business.center@vienna-hilton.telecomt.at, http://www.telecom.at/ViennaHilton

Sited close by the airport shuttle terminus, the Hilton lives up to the reputation of its international group. One floor is devoted to business travelers, and there is a well stocked shopping gallery. The north-facing rooms enjoy an interesting view over the Stadtpark and the historic city center.

Biedermeier im Sünnhof (37)
Landstrasse Hauptstrasse 28, 1030 ☎ (1) 71671-0 ➡ (1) 71671-503

Ⓜ Wienmitte 203 rooms ●●● 9 suites ▭ ▣ ☎ 🛗 ▥ 🍽 Terrassen-Restaurant, Zu den Deutschmeistern ▼ ✚ ✵ @ hotel.vienna@dorint.rogner.com, http://www.rogner.com

Another hotel close to the shuttle terminus, well sited for public transport and only 20 minutes on foot from the city center. The arcade-lined street with its rows of stores and smaller craft shops has recently been the object of a massive restoration project. The hotel itself is very intimate, comfortable and simply furnished in true Biedermeier style. Biedermeier derives from the name of an imaginary personage (literally 'Good Citizen Meier') symbolizing the tastes and values of the bourgeoisie who flourished in Austria in the first half of the 19th century.

Not forgetting

■ **Intercontinental (38)** Johannesgasse 28, 1037 Vienne
☎ (1) 71122-0 ➡ (1) 71344-89 ●●●● ■ **Sofitel Belvedere (39)**
Am Heumarkt 35-37, 1030 Vienne ☎ (1) 71616-0 ➡ (1) 71616-844 ●●●
■ **Starlight Suiten (40)** (➡ 30) Am Heumarkt 15, 1030
☎ (1) 535 9222 ➡ (1) 535 9222-11 ●●●

36

37

35

38

Landstr. Hauptstr.

Am Stadtpark

36

37

Wien

Gasse

Ungargasse

STADT-
PARK

Am Heumarkt

Linke Bahngasse

Rechte Bahngasse

Reisnerstrasse

Beatrixgasse

Tonlasse

U Stadtpark
Johannesg.

38 40

G. Keller-G.

Grimmelshausengasse

Salesianergasse

Neulinggasse

Strongasse

Am Heumarkt

Marokkanergasse

Jauresgasse

39

Zaunerg.-Traun-gasse

Schwarzen-
bergplatz

Rennweg

35

BELVEDERE

Despite
lacking the charm
of historic hotels,
the Intercontinental
has the advantage
of a good situation:
its front rooms
offer a panoramic
view over the
Stadtpark and the
Ring.

➡ Where to stay

Hotel Pension Schneider (41)
Getreidemarkt 5, 1060 ☎ (1) 58838-0 ➡ (1) 58838-212

M *Babenberger Strasse, Karlsplatz/Oper* **P** *35 rooms and apartments* ●● ▣
▣ ▣ ▣

The discreet appeal of this hotel is popular with opera singers. Who exactly? Look in the foyer, and you will see a display of photographs signed by many of these regular clients. The atmosphere is convivial, and the hotel is very well positioned between the Kunstakademie and the Theater an der Wien, with views of the Secession Building and the Naschmarkt. You can opt for a room or an apartment, whichever suits you; the latter will have a fully equipped kitchen. Both can be rented by the month.

Pension Kraml (42)
Brauergasse 5, 1060 ☎ (1) 587 8588 ➡ (1) 586 7573

M *Zieglergasse, Pilgramgasse* **14 rooms** ● ▣

This is a small pension, but well run and, value-wise, beats rivals hollow. You will find it in the immediate neighborhood of the Westbahnhof (Western railroad station). This means you will be staying only a brief walk from the shopping areas of the Mariahilferstrasse and the Flohmarkt, a small flea market open every Saturday morning. Within easy reach of the historic heart of Vienna by public transport.

Pension Hargita (43)
Andreasgasse 1, 1070 ☎ (1) 526 1928 ➡ (1) 526 0492

M *Zieglergasse* **10 rooms** ● ▣

You will like the price of the rooms, as well as the genial proprietress with her welcoming smile. This lady hails from Hungary, as the décor confirms! The place is spotless, incidentally. The Hargita is some ten minutes away from the Westbahnhof, at the end of the Mariastrasse, a long shopping street where all the big international names are found.

Kolping-Gästehaus (44)
Gumpendorfer Strasse 39 (entry by Stiegengasse 12), 1060
☎ (1) 587 5631-0 ➡ (1) 586 3630

M *U3 Neubaugasse, U4 Kettenbrückengasse* **P** *80 rooms* ● ▣ ▣ ▣ ▣

Should you be looking for a quiet room and a cheap bed for the night, try here. They don't promise luxuries or Jugendstil furniture, but the Kolping is friendly, well kept, respectable, practical – and even has its own little chapel.

Not forgetting

■ **Hotel Beethoven Best Western (45)** Millöckergasse 6, 1060
☎ (1) 5874482-0 ➡ (1) 587 4442 ●●● ■ **Astron Suite Hotel Wien
(46)** Mariahilfer Strasse 78, 1070 ☎ (1) 524 5600-0 ➡ (1) 524 560015 ●●●

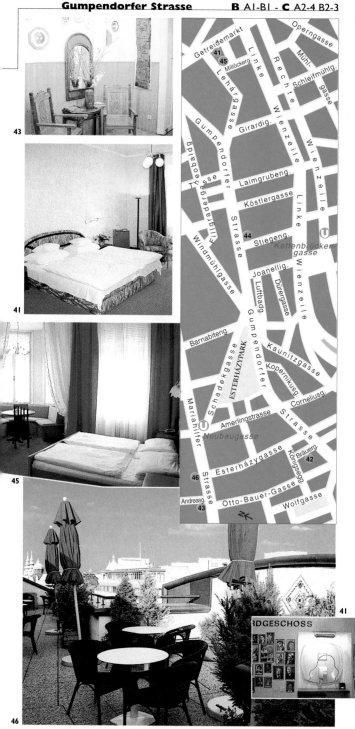

43

41

45

46

41

ERDGESCHOSS

35

In the area

- Where to eat: ➡ 54
- After dark: ➡ 78
- What to see: ➡ 104
- Where to shop: ➡ 130, 144 ➡ 148–149

Where to stay

Hotel-Pension Altstadt (47)

Kirchengasse 41, 1070 ☎ (1) 526 3399 ➡ 523 4901

P ***25 rooms*** ●● *6 suites* @ *alt.vie@magnet.at, http://members.magnet.at/users/alt.vie/*

This small hotel is the antithesis of the standard, impersonal establishment. It is an old 18th-century residence, its corridors and public rooms hung with works of art. The bedrooms, spacious and delightfully comfortable, are all personalized. All that remains is for you to choose between the *piano nobile*, with its pastel shades and stucco ceilings, and an attic room under the eaves. The service matches everything else, and the staff are exceptionally helpful.

K+K Maria Theresia (48)

Kirchberggasse 6-8, 1070 ☎ (1) 52123 ➡ (1) 521 2370

P ***123 rooms*** ●●● @ *kk.maria.theresia@kuk.at, http://www.kkhotels.com*

Here a restful atmosphere reigns in the attractive center of the Spillberg, which still recalls the not so distant past when it was the artists' quarter. There are innumerable small craft shops in the area and the main museums and the royal residence, the Hofburg, are only a stroll away. The rooms are up to all modern standards of comfort and even have air conditioning. Some also open onto a terrace.

Hotel Savoy (49)

Lindengasse 12, 1070 ☎ (1) 523 4646 ➡ (1) 523 4640

M *U3 Neubaugasse* P ***43 rooms*** ●●

What a difference between this place and the feverish activity of the big international chains! Here, the atmosphere is hushed, even cathedral-like. Reception staff will unfailingly help you with directions and invaluable advice.

Astron Suite-Hotel (50)

Lindengasse 9 (Mariahilfer Strasse 32-34), 1070
☎ (1) 52172-0 ➡ (1) 521 7215

M *U3 Neubaugasse* P *106 suites* ●●●
Astron Suite Hotel Wien Attersee *(46) Mariahilfer Strasse 78, 1070 ☎ (1) 524 5600-0 ➡ (1) 524 560015* @ *Wien@astron-hotels.de, http://www.asron-hotels.de*

Here, for the price of a room, you get a suite: bedroom, bathroom, living room with work area, kitchenette with microwave, all in contemporary décor. Two floors are reserved for non-smokers. And, yes, there is a fitness center and a sauna.

Not forgetting

- **Pension Reimer (51)** Kirchengasse 18, 1070 ☎ (1) 523 6162 ➡ (1) 524 3782 ●

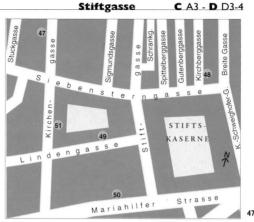

Tucked away in an 18th-century aristocrat's mansion, the Hotel-Pension Alstadt has preserved its prestige and old-world atmosphere: the bedrooms are tastefully furnished and works of art line the walls of the lounges.

47

47

50

51

49

Beiseln

These typical Viennese establishments are the equivalents of the French *bistro* and represent excellent value for money, serving generous helpings of the local fare.

Where to eat

Heurigen

These are far more than rustic inns among the vineyards: as well as eating and drinking you can listen to traditional music and enjoy wonderful views. The name derives from the word *heuriger*, meaning the season's new wine.

Something of everything

This is the very basis of Viennese cuisine, which draws upon recipes from Bohemia, Hungary, Poland, Italy… Desserts originating from medieval Burgundy or Constantinople, ice creams dreamed up in Trentino… with such ancestry no wonder the gastronomic tradition is constitutionally international! An essential item on most menus is beef in any of innumerable sauces; then there is the inexhaustible variety of pastries – also obtainable from the *Konditoreien* ➡ 82 – and aren't they irresistible!

Restaurants

THE INSIDER'S FAVORITES

◥ Where to eat

Palmenhaus (1)
Im Burggarten, 1010 ☎ (1) 533 1033

Ⓜ *U3 Volkstheater (exit Burgring). Entrance via Goethegasse or Burgring*
Mediterranean cuisine ⬛ ●●● ⬛ ⓢ *10–2am* ⬛ ⬛ ⬛ ⬛

Vienna will leave you with all sorts of memories. How about a summer
morning breakfast in a park, surrounded by lawns and trees? Unless, of
course, you prefer to lunch there – between taking in a couple of the
big museums, or to whet your appetite for them. The Palmenhaus is
located in the very heart of the Burggarten, facing the
Schmetterlinghaus. It has just undergone a facelift and offers light,
inventive cooking in refined surroundings. Its strong points: the hors
d'oeuvres, fish dishes and desserts.

Barbaro's (2)
Kärntner Strasse 19, 1010 (in the shopping mall)
☎ (1) 513 171220 ➡ (1) 513 1712

Ⓜ *U1, U3 Stephansplatz* **Multi-ethnic cuisine** ●●●● ⬛ ⬛ ⓢ *noon–4pm
and 6pm–1am* ⬛ ⬛ ⬛

An elevator designed to give panoramic views glides up the face of the
Steffl shopping mall. A first glimpse across the city, then you're looking
down with a bird's-eye view on the Stephansdom and the rooftops. The
atmosphere of Barbaro's is elegantly restrained, and its cuisine reveals
Asiatic and Italian influence. If necessary, you can wait comfortably in the
neighboring bar until your table is ready.

Piccini Piccolo Gourmet (3)
Linke Wienzeile 4, 1060 ☎ (1) 587 5254

Ⓜ *U4, U1, U2 Karlsplatz (exit: Secession)* **Italian cuisine** ⬛ ●●●
ⓢ *Mon.–Fri. 10.30am–7.30pm; Sat. 9am–2pm*

Vienna's most famous Italian restaurant can be discovered lurking
between the Secession Building, the Theater an der Wien and the
Naschmarkt. The menu boasts some delicious antipasti (hors d'oeuvre),
superb pâtés, fish soups, and, in the fall, the chef dreams up mouthwatering truffle recipes.

Korso (4)
Mahlerstrasse 2, 1010 ☎ (1) 515 16546 ➡ (1) 515 16575

Ⓜ *U4, U1, U2 Karlsplatz (exit Kärntnerstrasse)* **Traditional Viennese cuisine**
●●●●● ⬛ ⬛ ⓢ *Mon.–Fri. noon–2pm and 7–11pm* ⬛ ⬛

This miraculous establishment owes its existence to Reinhard Gerer,
one of Austria's most original chefs. He has kept all that was best in a
slightly faded hotel – the wonderful late 19th-century décor – and then
turned it into a restaurant with a magnet-like appeal for gourmets, locals
and visitors alike. The cuisine is subtly balanced, allying pure Viennese
tradition – *Tafelspitz* (boiled beef) or *Rieslingbeuschel* (lung stew made
with Riesling wine), for instance – with classic international dishes. Gerer
is a perfectionist: he has laid down a cellar brilliantly complementing his
artistry and keeps a very sharp eye on the standard of service. There is
also a pleasant bar where you can unwind.

STALLBURG

Plankengasse

Dorotheerg.

Spiegelg.

Neuer Markt

Himmelpfortg.

2

Josefs-platz

Augustinerstr.

Lobkowitz-platz

Tegetthoffstr.

Johannesg.

Annag.

Krugerstr.

1

BURG-GARTEN

Albertina-platz

Walfischg.

Goetheg.

Operng.

Mahlerstr.

4

Kärntner Strasse

Kärntner R.

O p e r n r i n g

E l i s a b e t h s t r a s s e

Schiller-platz

N i b e l u n g e n g a s s e

Karlsplatz

Makartg.

Operng.

Wiedner Hauptstr.

Karls-platz

Getreidemarkt

Linke Wienzeile

NASCHMARKT

Rechte Wienzeile

Millöckerg.

3

Operng. Wienzeile

3

PICCINI

R
Piccolo
PICCOLO GOURMET

PICCOLO GOURMET

2

4

4

In the area
- **Where to stay:** ➡ 24 ➡ 26 ➡ 28
- **After dark:** ➡ 70 ➡ 74 ➡ 78 ➡ 80 ➡ 82
- **What to see:** ➡ 88 ➡ 92
- **Where to shop:** ➡ 138-139 ➡ 140 ➡ 142 ➡ 144

Where to eat

Haas & Haas (5)
Stephansplatz 1, 1010 ☎ (1) 513 1916-0

 U3, U1 Stephansplatz *Sandwiches and patisseries* ▢ ●● ◷ *Mon.–Fri. 9am–8pm; Sat. 9am–6pm* ▣ ▦ ✦

No longer merely a tearoom where they serve brioches and *tramezzini* (sandwiches), Haas have gone along with more typical Viennese influences. They have extended their range and now also serve delicious cakes and light snacks, accompanied by the inevitable coffee. In summer, you can sit outside in the shadow of the cathedral.

Trzesniewski (6)
Dorotheergasse 1, 1010 ☎ (1) 512 3291

▣ U1, U2, U3 Stephansplatz *Aufstrichbrot* ▢ ● ◷ *Mon.–Fri. 8.30am–7.30pm; Sat. 9am–5pm*

Half-Polish, half-Viennese eatery where they serve exclusively *Aufstrichbrot*, a sort of open sandwich topped with tasty chicken liver pâté, or garnished with *speck* (bacon), eggs, crawfish or herring ... with a touch of spice to give it some bite.

Do & Co (7)
Stephansplatz 12, 1010 ☎ (1) 535 3969 ➡ (1) 535 3959

▣ U1, U3 Stephansplatz *International cuisine* ●●●● ▭ ▮▮ ◷ *noon–3pm, 6pm–midnight* ▥ ▼ ⚹ ✦

There's no denying Do & Co is one of the top reastaurants: the place is perched at the top of Hans Hollein's great glass palace opposite the Stephansdom. What's more, the chef, Attila Dougan, who has a formidable reputation, supplies airlines, and even uses airplanes – particularly from the firm owned by Niki Lauda, the former racing champion – to bring in supplies of lobsters and oysters!

Drei Husaren (8)
Weihburggasse 4, 1010 ☎ (1) 512 1092 ➡ (1) 512 1092-18

▣ U1, U3 Stephansplatz *Viennese gourmet cuisine* ●●●●● ▭ ▮▮ ◷ *noon–3pm and 6pm–1am* ▥ ▰ ▼

This is the capital's oldest luxury restaurant, with an aristocratic ambiance and traditional cuisine. Its hors d'oeuvre carts are the stuff of legend. The house *Husarenbeuschel* (variety meats) and *Husarenpfannkuchen* (omelet) are prepared from 'grandma's recipes' but are very refined. The fish dishes and desserts? Unforgettable.

Not forgetting

■ **Weibels Wirtshaus (9)** Kumpfgasse 2, 1010 ☎ (1) 512 3986 ▣ U3 Stubenbastei **Creative cuisine** ▢ ●● ▭ ◷ *Mon.–Sat. 11.30am–11.30pm* ✦ *Tasty dishes to wash down with one of their good wines. Very enjoyable atmosphere. If full, try* **Weibels Bistro***, Riemergasse 1-3, 1010 ☎ (01) 513 3110.* ■ **A Tavola (10)***, Weihburggasse 3-5, 1010 ☎ (1) 512 7955,* ▣ U1,U3 Stephansplatz *Italian cuisine* ▢ ●●● ▭ ◷ *Mon.–Sat. noon–2pm and 6–11pm* ⚹ *Plain, good cooking with the accent on country style. Excellent choice of wines.*

➡ Where to eat

Oswald & Kalb (11)
Bäckerstrasse 14, 1010 ☎ (1) 512 1371 ➡ (1) 512 1371

Ⓜ *U3 Stubentor (exit Wollzeile)* **Viennese and Styrian cuisine** ●●● ▭
🕐 *6pm–2am* Ⓨ

In the Middle Ages, it was in this area, around the Alte Universität, that students met up to have a good time. The last thirty or so years have seen an explosion in the numbers of *Beiseln* or typical Viennese bistrots – yet Oswald & Kalb is rightly reckoned to be the original. The atmosphere is extremely cordial, attracting students and intellectuals who still like to get together over a salad dressed with pumpkin seed oil from Styria or a leg of lamb washed down with a good glass of sparkling Schilcher.

Neu Wien (12)
Bäckerstrasse 5, 1010 ☎ (1) 513 0666

Ⓜ *U1, U3 Stephansplatz* **Mediterranean cuisine** ●●● ▭ 🕐 *6pm–1am*

The local intelligentsia have set up headquarters in this splendid vaulted room enlivened with Modernist paintings by Christian Ludwig Attersee – a regular diner here. The food is principally Mediterranean, but with a light touch. Extensive wine list. Right next door is the bar, a favorite roosting-place for Vienna's night-owls.

Plachutta (13)
Wollzeile 38, 1010 ☎ (1) 512 1577 ➡ (1) 512 1577-20

Ⓜ *U3 Stubentor* **Traditional Viennese beef cuisine** ●●●● ▭ 🍴
🕐 *11.30am–2.30pm and 6–10pm* ▣

The Plachutta family maintains the Viennese tradition of beef-based cuisine in three different city restaurants. In the Wollzeile, with its mixed period and modern décor, priority is given to soups and *Tafelspitz* (boiled beef) served with its portion of vegetables. But fish-lovers won't feel let down; the fish is always fresh, the dishes subtle and creative. Like all self-respecting Viennese restaurants, the Plachutta serves great desserts: some of the house specials are the famous *meringues à la Chantilly*, rhubarb strudel and semolina gateau in a raspberry coulis. The wine list contains some refined Viennese whites, including the 'Wiener Trilogie', from the Wieninger vineyards.

Vis à Vis (14)
Wollzeile 5, 1010 ☎ (1) 512 9350

Ⓜ *U1, U3 Stephansplatz* **Wine bar** ▰ ● 🕐 *Mon.–Fri. 3–10.30pm*

This wine bar is tiny, always full to bursting, and is a first-rate example of a Viennese *Beisl*. These popular bistros, often family-run, offer simple, tasty and homely cooking at a fair price. However, they are often closed in the evenings and at weekends... But guess what: Vis à Vis is an exception! In its unostentatious surroundings, it serves excellent hors d'oeuvre based around ham, mortadella, cheese and olives, which you can help down with one of the delicious white wines served by the glass.

In the traditional Viennese *Beisl* or bistrot – the field is led by Oswald and Kalb – you can buy wine by the glass and try the local fare, which is simple but tasty.

In the area
- **Where to stay:** ➡ 26
- **After dark:** ➡ 80 ➡ 82
- **What to see:** ➡ 92 ➡ 96 ➡ 98 ➡ 100 ➡ 102 ➡ 114–115
- **Where to shop:** ➡ 138–139 ➡ 146 ➡ 148–149

➡ Where to eat

Bei Max (15)
Landhausgasse 2/Herrengasse 9, 1010 ☎ (1) 533 7359

Ⓜ U3 Herrengasse **Carinthian cuisine** ⬛ ●● 🕐 Mon.–Fri. 11am–10pm

Now here's a chance to (quite literally) stuff yourself with *Käsnudeln* and *Kletzennudeln*, typical dumplings filled with cheese or fruit. The Bei Max also goes in for Viennese menus, with both traditional and country-style fare. Draft Carinthian beer, palatable wines and some powerful *Schnaps*.

Schwarzes Kameel (16)
Bognergasse 5, 1010 ☎ (1) 5338967

Ⓜ U1, U3 Stephansplatz **Hors d'oeuvre and Viennese cuisine** ●/●●● ▭
🕐 Mon.–Fri. 8.30am–8pm; Sat. 8.30am–3pm 🕐 restaurant noon–3pm 🍸

Here is a place with a history: Beethoven, for instance, used to come here often. There is a delicatessen selling superb *charcuterie*, plus cold dishes and sandwiches for eating at the bar or taking away. The Jugendstil-style restaurant concocts traditional Viennese meals. If you are a fan of Brötchen (rolls), turn up to the back of the shop on Saturday morning in company with all the youth and beauty of Vienna. It's a hard job pushing through the throng precariously balancing your plate and a glass of white wine! Never mind, there is a chance of a great conversation any moment. This place boasts a deep cellar, a real treasure trove, where connoisseurs assemble for some spirited tasting sessions...

Kecks feine Kost (17)
Herrengasse 15, 1010 ☎ (1) 533 6367

Ⓜ U3 Herrengasse **Hors d'oeuvre** ⬛ ● 🕐 Mon.–Fri. 9am–6.30pm 🔲 🔲

This is undoubtedly the best spot in Vienna to judge Austrians' flair in matters gastronomical, especially since there are some notable wines on offer too. If you have any lingering doubts, you can taste (as much as you like) before buying. Mouthwatering salads, flans, gateaux, and, every Wednesday, wonderful *Weisswürste*, which resemble Bavarian sausages.

È Tricaffè (18)
Am Hof 2/Bognergasse 4, 1010 ☎ (1) 533 8490 ➡ (1) 533 8490

Ⓜ U3 Herrengasse **Italian cuisine** ●●● ▭ 🕐 Mon.–Sat. 8am–midnight
🕐 snack bar 11.30am–2.30pm, 6–11pm 🔲 🍸 ♿

Designed in the best Italian taste, this eating-house is halfway between snack bar and restaurant, with a laid-back, happy ambience. Scrumptious sandwiches, memorable hors d'oeuvre, meat and fish dishes with great flavorings, including sea-perch with thyme and *paupiettes à la rue* (paupiettes garnished with a lightly peppered green salad). The only reservation is that the wine list is rather sparse. But the owners must have got it right: their formula has been a smash-hit in Vienna ... They are expecting to open a second restaurant shortly, in the city center, opposite the cathedral.

➡ Where to eat

Hansen (19)
Wipplinger Strasse 34, 1010 ☎ (1) 532 0542 ➡ (1) 532 0542-10

Ⓜ U2, U4 Schottenring *Creative cuisine* ●●● ▢ 🔖 🕐 Mon.–Fri. 9am–8pm;
Sat. 9am–5pm 🐾 🍽 🌿

Customers arriving from the Ring are greeted by the scent of flowers
and a luxuriant forest of foliage: the Lederleitner Garden Center has
taken up its abode under the arcades. Hansen, in accordance with the
spirit of the place, serves light, resourceful dishes which will go down
well with those who have to watch their waistlines – each plateful is
really a half-portion. The wine list has been carefully compiled, even if it
does seem a bit brief. At Hansen, you can even eat breakfast under the
palm trees. At midday the kitchen is turned over to the preparation of
imaginative lunches blending Viennese tradition with influences from the
Mediterranean or Asia. No wonder the place is popular. The only
drawback is that the restaurant shuts at 8pm: the same time as the
Garden Center. So, in the evening, you have only time for a quick bite
before your opera or show begins. Unless, of course, you go out and buy
oil, vinegar, preserves and pasta, and throw together a little something in
your lodgings!

Fadinger (20)
Wipplinger Strasse 29, 1010 ☎ (1) 533 4341

Ⓜ U2 Schottenring *Viennese cuisine* 🔲 ●●● 🕐 Mon.–Fri. 11am–3pm,
5.30–10pm

The lord and master of this quiet little restaurant, which is somewhat off
the beaten track, is one of Vienna's most original chefs, Josef Fadinger,
whose trademark is attention to detail. Until a few years back he slaved
at the stove in a very up-market restaurant. Now he runs his own place,
and delights in tickling the palates of the chosen few who get to reserve
a table.

Salzamt (21)
Ruprechtsplatz 1, 1010 ☎ (1) 533 5332

Ⓜ U1, U4 Schwedenplatz *Viennese and Mediterranean cuisine* ●●●
🕐 5pm–1am; Sun. 5pm–2am 🍸 🕐 5pm–4am ⭐ 🌿

In the heart of Vienna's oldest quarter is an area known to the modern
generation as 'The Bermuda Triangle'. This is where it all happens after
dark. Epicures, artists, architects and the lesser lights of the fashion
world meet at the Salzamt to enjoy the excellent Viennese cooking with
its touch of the Mediterranean. The surroundings are chic but restrained,
the terrace pleasant to say the least, and the wines are light and lively.

Lustig Essen (22)
Salvatorgasse 6/Marc-Aurel-Strasse, 1010 ☎ (1) 533 3037

Ⓜ U1, U3 Stephansplatz *Creative cuisine* ●● ▢ 🕐 11.30am–midnight

This is the place if you want a bite to eat but cannot make up your mind
what to have. They serve small portions which let you try out a whole
range of hors d'oeuvres, main dishes and desserts. For jaded gourmets in
search of revelations, or the nibblers and peckers of this world.

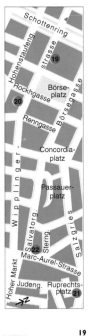

19

19

22

22

The plethora of hors d'oeuvre, main dishes and desserts allow the Lustig Essen's customers to try an unusual range of specialties in a single evening.

20

In the area

➡ **Where to stay:** ➡ 26 ➡ 30
➡ **After dark:** ➡ 68 ➡ 72 ➡ 76 ➡ 78 ➡ 80 ➡ 82
➡ **What to see:** ➡ 98 ➡ 110
➡ **Where to shop:** ➡ 138–139 ➡ 146 ➡ 148–149

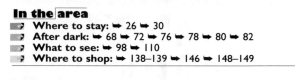

➡ **Where to eat**

Stein's Diner (23)
Kolingasse 1, 1090 ☎ (1) 310 9515

Ⓜ *U2 Schottenring* **International cuisine** 🔲 ●● Ⓢ *Mon.–Sat. 7pm–1am* 🅨 🔳

Stein's has found a home in the cellar of a student café. Its décor is modern and minimalist, and it offers a sophisticated menu blending Viennese and Mediterranean traditions reinterpreted in an Asian fashion. In the same spirit, Ossi Schellman, the owner, runs the 'Summer Stage', to be found on the bank of the Donaukanal, near the Rossauerlande station (subway line U4).

Stomach (24)
Seegasse 26, 1090 ☎ (1) 310 2099

Ⓜ *U4 Rossauer Lände* **Austrian cuisine** 🔲 ●● Ⓢ *Wed.–Sat. 6pm–midnight; Sun. noon–10pm* 🔳

'Stomach' may be an anagram of the former owner's name, but its other meaning is plain: your stomach will not be disappointed here. The cooking, always light-handed, is done with flair; only quality ingredients are used, brought in directly from the country's agricultural co-operatives. What is more, the prices have not run wild!

Elsässer Bistro (25)
Währingerstrasse 32, 1090 ☎ (1) 319 7689 ➡ (1) 417 5714

Ⓜ *U2 Schottenring* **Alsatian cuisine** 🔲 ●●● Ⓢ *noon–2.30pm and 6–9pm* 🔳 🔳

Thomas Seiler, a native of Alsace, had the idea of installing a restaurant in the old kitchens of the Palais Clam Gallas, home of the Cultural Institute and the École Française. In summer, he sets out rustic tables in the little garden, where clients can enjoy tripe with a piquant sauce or quails in a *sauce madère*, all washed down with Alsatian wines. Thomas Seiler's gastronomic philosophy is based on an aversion to unnecessary eccentricity: what counts is that food is appetizing. He stakes his reputation on the freshness of his ingredients, bringing out their quality in recipes inspired by the finest bistrot traditions. He particularly excels in fish and seafood platters. The desserts clearly reveal their creator's French origins: his *crème caramel* is a dream! Though Vienna has assimilated every kind of ethnic cuisine, French gastronomic cooking is rather under-represented. This surely explains the Elsässer's success with gourmets who are also francophiles. Reasonable prices, too.

Zur Goldenen Kugel (26)
Lazarettgasse 6 ☎ (1) 405 8363

Ⓜ *U6 Alserstrasse* **Viennese cuisine** 🔲 ●●● Ⓢ *Thu.–Mon. 9am–3pm and 6–11pm* 🔳 🔳

This authentic *Beisl* still offers true Viennese cooking with quality beers and good Austrian wines. It is hardly surprising, then, that the doctors from the nearby hospital make a point of meeting here after work. The interior garden is very attractive, as is the room reserved for non-smokers and the children's play area. Viennese tradition demands that pride of place is given to beef dishes and desserts.

A large reconstruction program has turned the site of the old hospital into a university campus. Students like to meet up at the many stores, *Beiseln*, cybercafés and discos in the lush setting of lawns and trees.

In the area

- **Where to stay:** ➡ 26, 30 ➡ 36
- **After dark:** ➡ 68 ➡ 72 ➡ 76 ➡ 78 ➡ 82
- **What to see:** ➡ 98 ➡ 104 ➡ 114–115
- **Where to shop:** ➡ 138–139 ➡ 146 ➡ 148–149

➡ Where to eat

Selina (27)
Laudongasse 13, 1080 ☎ (1) 405 6404 ➡ (1) 408 0459

Ⓜ U2 *Rathaus* **Austrian creative cuisine** ●●●● ▤ 🍴 🕐 11.30am–2pm, 6–11pm 🔲

The décor of the Selina is based on an alternation of black and white, with only the flowers adding a touch of color. In such sophisticated surroundings they serve some imaginative food: fish dishes and Austrian recipes biased toward country fare with some clever innovations, like grilled and spiced sucking-pig, *Grammelknödel* (dumplings stuffed with pork *rillons*), *Tafelspitz* (boiled beef) topped with potatoes… A pity the desserts are not really a house specialty. Polite, efficient service.

Prinz Ferdinand (28)
Bennoplatz 2, 1080 ☎ (1) 402 9417 ➡ (1) 402 9417

Ⓜ U6 *Josefstädterstrasse* **Viennese cuisine** ●● ▤ 🕐 Tue.–Sun. 11.30am–2.45pm, 6–10.45pm ✴

This picture-postcard *Beisl* (bistrot) is housed in a remarkable Biedermeier building. In summer, it spreads its wings outdoors into the garden. The menu contains all the classic Viennese dishes (boiled beef, fried chicken, grilled lamb's liver…), while making the occasional foray – not entirely successfully – into international cuisine. On the other hand, the desserts are sure-fire hits, despite taking a few liberties with traditional Austrian recipes. Wide selection of wines and liquors.

Schnattl (29)
Langegasse 40, 1080 ☎ (1) 405 3400 ➡ (1) 405 3400

Ⓜ U2 *Josefstädterstrasse* **Austrian creative cuisine, Austrian style** ●●● ▤ 🕐 Mon.–Fri. 11.30am–3pm and 6–11pm; Sat. 6–11pm ✴

Schnattl's is tucked away in the heart of the Josefstadt, the home of the Viennese bourgeoisie, very near the Theater in der Josefstadt founded by Max Reinhardt. The cuisine is in harmony with the ambience of the district: attached to tradition, but ready to experiment with the less conventional. The menu reveals Mediterranean influences, but these are variations on Austrian recipes: rue salad with shavings of Parmesan, *Knödels* (dumplings) stuffed with smoked fish, cabbage soup with potato quarters, ribs of venison with celery-filled ravioli… High quality wine list, with Austrian and international vintages.

Neues Rathaus (30)
Florianigasse 2, 1080 ☎ (01) 408 0112

Ⓜ U2 Josefstädterstrasse (exit Rathaus) **Austrian cuisine** ●●● ▤ 🕐 Mon.–Fri. 11am–midnight. 🔲 🔲 ✴

A select band of Austrian middle-class professionals (including judges and lawyers from the neighboring courthouse) gathers here over a good meal. Variety of local specialties, but the prices are a bit steep.

FLORIANIPARK

Wickenburggasse

Schlösselgasse

Tulpeng.

Lammgasse

Laudongasse

Lange Gasse

SCHÖNBORN-PARK

Florianigasse

M.-Treu-G.

Kochgasse

Piaristeng.

Jodok-Fink-Platz

Lederergasse

Fuhrmannsgasse

Florianigasse

Schönborngasse

Kupkagasse

Skodagasse

Hamer-lingpl.

Strasse

Lercheng.

Florianigasse

Albert-

Josefstädter

Tigergasse

Benno-pl.

gasse

Bennog.

Gasthaus zum Prinz Ferdinand

27

30

28

29

In the area

➡ **Where to stay:** ➡ 36
➡ **After dark:** ➡ 76 ➡ 78
➡ **What to see:** ➡ 104 ➡ 114–115
➡ **Where to shop:** ➡ 130 ➡ 138–139 ➡ 144 ➡ 148–149

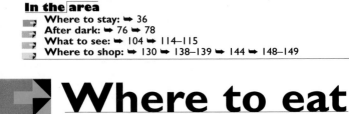

Where to eat

Beim Novak (31)
Richtergasse 12, 1070 ☎ (1) 522 23244

Ⓜ U3 Neubaugasse *Austrian cuisine* ●●● ▭ 🕐 *Mon.–Fri. 11.30am–3pm, 6–11pm; Sat. 5–11pm; closed public holidays* ▼

Novak's is in an area where wealthy industrialists once had their homes, now the domain of the big newspaper corporations. The red wood in the restaurant's vast dining room lends it a note of warmth, while plants and flowers harmonize with the flourishing courtyard garden, accessible through the French doors. In these simple and straightforward surroundings they serve traditional dishes, while not averse to experimentation. There is a smaller room which can be hired for private functions.

Zu ebener Erde und erster Stock (32)
Burggasse 13, 1070 ☎ (1) 523 6254

Ⓜ U3 Volkstheater Ⓟ *Creative cuisine* ●●●● ▭ 🕐 *Tue.–Fri. noon–2.30pm, 6–11.30pm; Sat. 6–11.30pm*

The old quarter of Spittelberg draws out the Viennese after dark. This is no recent phenomenon; they were coming here from the 18th century to hear the singers. Nowadays they come for the taverns. The area, with its large artist population, is no less crowded during the day, when people flock here to poke around in the little craft markets, especially during Advent. Its popularity is unlikely to decline, since it will soon be directly linked with the Museum Quarter destined to house collections of modern Viennese art. The Zu ebener Erde und erster Stock – 'Ground and First Floor', alluding to the title of a play by Austrian dramatist Nestroy – has squeezed itself into a tiny Biedermeier building; you eat on the ground floor, the first floor is the bar. Customers are carefully cosseted, and the cooking is sophisticated and subtle.

Grünauer (33)
Hermanngasse 32, 1070 ☎ (1) 526 4080 ➡ (1) 526 1419

Ⓜ U3 Neubaugasse *Austrian cuisine* 🍴 ●● 🕐 *Tue.–Fri. 11.30am–2.30pm, Mon.–Fri. 6–10.30pm*

This old establishment with its wood paneling and spartan furnishings is the culinary domain of a woman chef. Here she reinvents classic Viennese cuisine by blending yesterday's flavors with today's. Best book ahead, as the place is popular with gourmets and patronized by the arts and media fraternity. Excellent selection of wines and liquors.

Al Cappello (34)
Hermanngasse 30, 1070 ☎ (1) 524 6888 ➡ (1) 602 0951

Ⓜ U3 Neubaugasse *Friuli cuisine* ●●● ▭ 🕐 *Mon.–Sat. 5–11pm*

Taste the food here and you immediately think of the Italian province on the borders of Austria and Slovenia: Friuli, with its mountain-style cuisine which complements the Venetian preference for seafood. The *antipasti* (hors d'oeuvre) are irresistible, as are the stews and the soups seasoned with herbs. The region's famous names figure strongly on the wine list. Tuesdays and Wednesdays, scrumptious grills are prepared over a wood fire.

Italian cuisine is
prized in Vienna.

➤ Where to eat

Schwarzer Adler (35)
Schönbrunnerstrasse 40, 1050 ☎ (1) 544 1109 ➡ (1) 544 1109

Ⓜ U4 Pilgramgasse **Viennese cuisine** ●●● ▢ Ⓥ Tue.–Sat. 11am–2.30pm, 6–11pm ✴

The dishes typical of Viennese gourmet cuisine are prepared here with competence and skill, but the Mediterranean is never far away. Side by side with *Butterschnitzel* (escalope of veal in butter) you will find ravioli stuffed with mushrooms or Italian cheese, and, rubbing shoulders with Austrian wines, many a bottle of Italian. The range of beers is absolutely remarkable. And especially, don't try and resist the mouthwatering cakes! You will appreciate the warm, family atmosphere of this place; don't hesitate to ask for advice from the waiters who will tactfully and expertly recommend dishes not displayed on the menu, and the best wines to go with them.

Zu den drei Buchteln (36)
Wehrgasse 9, 1050 ☎ (1) 587 8365

Ⓜ U4 Kettenbrückengasse **Bohemian cuisine** 🔲 ●● Ⓥ Mon.–Sat. 6–11pm

Typical, tasty Bohemian platters: *Krautfleckerln* (pasta squares and cabbage) and *Topfenhaluska* (gnocchi stuffed with curd cheese and sprinkled with pork scratchings), dumplings – with meat or pork fillings – *Liwanzen* (crepes spread with prune jam) and *Powidltascherln*. These will taste all the better with a bottle of Bohemian wine or beer, of which there is a great choice.

Bevanda (37)
Wehrgasse 8, 1050 ☎ (1) 587 4266

Ⓜ U4 Kettenbrückengasse **Fish cuisine** ●●●● ▢ Ⓥ Sun.–Fri. 6pm–midnight; closed Sun., July–Aug ▮

An unpretentious, hospitable restaurant, with an impressive Mediterranean menu. The fish is particularly appetizing; it is always fresh, and cooked to traditional Italian and Dalmatian recipes. These countries also provide the mainstay of the wine list, but you will find some of the better Austrian varieties as well, and your charming hostess will not be parsimonious with good advice and useful suggestions. You absolutely *must* try the Sekt Bründlmayer, which, it is claimed, is the equal of any French champagne – and it's cheaper! This is the rendezvous for Viennese who love fish cuisine, even if the prices are a bit steep. You get what you pay for, in Vienna as anywhere else.

Green Cottage (38)
Kettenbrückengasse 3, 1050 ☎ (1) 586 6581 ➡ (1) 586 6581-4

Ⓜ U4 Kettenbrückengasse **Chinese cuisine** 🔲 ●●● Ⓥ Mon.–Sat. 6–11.30pm ✴

This is Vienna's most creative Chinese restaurant. The atmosphere is modern and plush, the food a lively blend of tradition and innovation: duck in piquant sauce, medallions of smoked venison served on tea leaves, rice balls with ginger… And if you can't forego a glass of wine with your meal, there's a very respectable choice.

In the area
■→ **Where to stay:** ➡ 20 ➡ 32
■→ **After dark:** ➡ 66 ➡ 74 ➡ 76
■→ **What to see:** ➡ 112
■→ **Where to shop:** ➡ 130 ➡ 138-139 ➡ 148-149

■► Where to eat

Palais Schwarzernberg (39)
Schwarzenbergplatz 9, 1030 ☎ (1) 798 4515 ➡ (1) 798 4714

Ⓜ *U1, U2, U4 Karlsplatz* 🅿 *International gastronomic cuisine* ●●●●● ▭
🍴 ⏱ *noon–2.30pm, 6–10.30pm* ▥ 🎵 🖾 🍷 🍸 ★ 🏔

A palace overlooking an immense Baroque park: just the place if you
dream of high society and the very best food. All the famous dishes of
mainstream international cuisine are to be found here, skillfully prepared
from the finest ingredients; for instance, the fish are caught directly on
the estates of Prince Schwarzenberg. The service is stylish but
unaffected; after all, the owner cultivates a deliberately unpretentious
image as a simple countryman and tavern-keeper! There is a parking lot
for customers at the front entrance. Near the restaurant there is a
congenial bar where, in winter, you can enjoy your drink in front of the
flickering wood fire. Various rooms in the palace – complete with period
furniture and old paintings – can be hired for private functions. You will
also enjoy a stroll in the park adjoining the Belvedere; with its sculptures
and little lakes, it's an oasis of peace amid the tumult of the city.

Gusshaus (40)
Gusshausstrasse 23, 1040 ☎ (1) 504 4750 ➡ (1) 504 9464

Ⓜ *U1, U2, U4 Karlsplatz* **Creative cuisine** ●●● ▭ ⏱ *Mon.–Fri. 11am–
2.30pm, 6–11pm; Sat. 6–10pm* ★

Now here is a *Beisl* with plenty of surprises. You can try out Viennese
and Mediterranean specialties in simple but hospitable and pleasing
surroundings. There is also a gastronomic menu at uninflated prices. The
wines, liquors and draft beers are thoughtfully chosen and complement
the food in quality. In summer you can eat on the terrace, and there is a
small room for private functions.

Demi Tass (41)
Prinz Eugenstrasse 28, 1040 ☎ (1) 504 3119

Ⓜ *U1 Taubstummengasse* **French and Indian cuisine** ●●●● ▭
⏱ *Mon.–Sat. 11.30am–2pm, 6–11.30pm* ♿

This establishment has founded its own tradition of culinary
intermarriage! French and Indian cuisines have been harmoniously
integrated, so you will find classic French gastronomic dishes side by side
with tasty, spicy offerings from the Indian repertoire. You won't regret a
visit; it makes an exciting and unusual evening out.

Bodega Española (42)
Belvederegasse 10, 1040 ☎ 504 5500, ➡ 587 9700

Ⓜ *U1 Taubstummengasse* **Spanish cuisine** 🍴 ●●● ⏱ *Tue.–Sat.
6pm–midnight*

Tapas to suit every taste: this is the specialty of this agreeable
establishment, popular with the Spanish community. Obviously, they
serve the famous *pata negra* (a ham dish), traditional meat and fish
dishes and the inevitable *crème brûlée*… not to mention the wines and
liquors, which are all top quality.

39

40

41

40

42

In the area
➡ **Where to stay:** ➡ 32
➡ **After dark:** ➡ 66 ➡ 74
➡ **What to see:** ➡ 90 ➡ 106–107 ➡ 112 ➡ 114–115
➡ **Where to shop:** ➡ 130 ➡ 140 ➡ 148–149

Where to eat

Zum alten Heller (43)
Ungargasse 34, 1030 ☎ (1) 712 6452

Ⓜ U3 *Rochusmarkt* **Viennese cuisine** 🔲 ●●● Ⓞ 11.30am–10pm 🟥

This restaurant serves an amazing variety of roasts and ragouts, proof if ever one were needed of the Viennese passion for beef dishes. This is *the* place to explore *bürgerliche Küche* – literally, 'bourgeois cooking': boiled beef, huge portions of meat, lavish gateaux. Remember that any item can be served as a 'child's portion'. In good weather you can eat in the courtyard under the shade of some very old trees.

Steirereck (44)
Rasumofskygasse 2, 1030 ☎ (1) 713 3168 ➡ (1) 713 31682

Ⓜ U3 *Rochusmarkt* **Austrian gastronomic cuisine** ●●●●● 🔲 🍴
Ⓞ *Mon.–Fri. noon–3pm, 7–11pm*

Vienna's premier restaurant is located outside the center, on the road leading to the Prater. The owner comes from Styria, and Styrian fare is therefore preeminent. None of the offerings will disappoint, however, and the staff are smiling and efficient. Here you can indulge yourself at any hour. Breakfast might be a *Gabelfrühstück*, a gargantuan platter of Viennese specialties; for lunch, try the tasty *Mittagsmenu*; in the evening, after the show, there is the memorable *Restelessen*. So be tempted by the oysters with ginger, the beef *à la mode de Styrie*, something from the selection of gateaux, or the *Griesschmarm* (baked semolina pudding). The cheese platter and the wine list are worth a good look; there is a particularly fine dessert wine to complement the archetypal Austrian cheeses: Alois Kracher's Süsswein, from the Burgenland, familiar the world over.

Academie (45)
Untere Viaduktegasse 45, 1030 ☎ (1) 713 8256 ➡ (1) 713 8257

Ⓜ U4, U3 *Landstrasse* **Creative gastronomic cuisine** ●●●●● 🔲 🍴
Ⓞ *Mon.–Fri. noon –2.30pm, 7–10.30pm* 🔲

Chef Meinrad Neunkirchen is a past master in the art of subtly blending tastes and aromas, with the inimitable flavors of his creations deriving from essences of herbs and flowers. Some examples from the menu: fried sardines with sweet-and-sour gherkins and dandelions, or lamb's liver with starwort. His recipes are often weird but wonderful, and your palate will probably return a favorable verdict.

Dubrovnik (46)
Am Heumarkt 5, 1030 ☎ (1) 713 2755

Ⓜ U4 *Stadtpark* **Balkan cuisine** ●●● 🔲 Ⓞ *Mon.–Fri. 11.30am–3pm, 5.30pm–midnight; open all day Sun. and public holidays.* 🎵

Traditional cooking is only part of a whole intriguing, deliberately contrived atmosphere of wistfulness and nostalgia. Every evening, while the staff prepare fish from the Adriatic, delicious grills, or hors d'oeuvres redolent of aromatic herbs, a pianist plays nostalgic melodies from days gone by.

ZUM ALTEN HELLER

The Dubrovnik is the place for Balkan atmosphere and specialties. The capital of the old Austro-Hungarian empire remains a cultural melting-pot.

KAISER BIER

RESTAURANT
DUBROVNIK

61

Vienna has its own wine-making industry. Amongst the rolling, vine-clad hills locals fete the arrival of a new light white wine (*Heuriger*) at one of the *Heurigen* or village taverns. Here they serve hearty country meals buffet-style: lentils in pork fat, roast pork, local ham …

➡ Where to eat

Kierlinger (47)
Kahlenbergerstrasse 20, 1190 ☎ (1) 372264

M *U4 Heiligenstadt* ▣ ● 🕓 *3.30pm–midnight; Sun. till 11pm* ✶

Since 1787 this inn has been owned by the Kierlkinger family, famous for the quality of Rheinriesling and Weissburgunder grapes grown in its vineyards. You can drink at the bar, in a relaxed and happy atmosphere, or find a table in one of the dining-rooms or in the garden under the shade of limes and chestnut trees. The self-service buffet is first-class; there are hot and cold meat dishes, but don't forget to try the *Liptauer*, a kind of spread made of fresh cheese flavored with herbs. This is the house specialty, and the recipe is passed down from one generation to the next.

Sirbu (48)
Kahlenbergerstrasse 210, 1190 ☎ (1) 320 5928

M *U4 Heiligenstadt* ▣ ▣ ● ▭ 🕓 *Apr 1.–mid-Oct.: Mon.–Sat. 3pm–midnight* ✶ ▨

Perched up on the Nussberg, the Sirbu offers an outstanding view over the Kahlenberg and the Leopoldsberg: you can see the Danube and all the northern district of Vienna. You can dine on the terrace, but it is just as appealing inside. All the wines are excellent, but you may prefer the Nussdorfer Riesling. There is a buffet offering traditional peasant dishes, including some organic recipes.

Mayer am Pfarrplatz (49)
Pfarrplatz 2, 1190 ☎ (1) 370 1287

M *U4 Heiligenstadt* ● ▭ 🕓 *4pm–midnight; Sun. and public holidays 11am–midnight* ✶

In 1817, while staying in this building, Beethoven wrote his Ninth Symphony. Today, this is the home of one of Vienna's most acclaimed restaurants, where the most select wines are served. Three to remember in particular are the Nussberger, Alsegger Riesling and Traminer. The area is swarming with eating places, each with a garden where you can taste the vintages after a visit to the cellars. The engineer Hans Mayer, who runs the inn with his family, is a pioneer of high-quality Viennese wine-growing; the results are remarkable, and his 'Vienna Classic' has made Vienna's name in the wine world.

Oppolzer (50)
Himmelstrasse 22, 1190 ☎/➡ (1) 322 4160

Ⓜ U4 Heiligenstadt 🔲 ● 🕑 *5pm–midnight; closed Sun. and public holidays* ✖

One of the smartest establishments in Grinzing, with a recommendable buffet, splendid wines and a delightful garden.

Zimmermann (51)
Armbrustergasse 77, 1190 ☎ (1) 320 5818

Ⓜ U4 Heiligenstadt ● ▤ 🕑 *5pm–midnight; closed Sun. and public holidays* ✖

This is the inn to come to for a happy if unconventional evening out. Still and sparkling wines from the Klosterneuburg Reserve accompanied by well prepared food.

After dark

Festivals

January: *Resonanzen* (ancient music).

April: *Osterlang* (classical music).

May-June: *Wiener Festwochen* (classical music, dance, theater, opera).

July: *Puls Tanz, Internazionale Tanzwochen Wien* (contemporary dance). Also *Jazz fest Wien*.

July-August: *Klangbogen* (classical music, opera); *Mozart in Schönbrunn* (Mozart operas).

October: *Wien Modern* (Contemporary music); *Viennale* (cinema).

Information and reservations

Information on shows and cultural events in Vienna can be obtained on the Internet (http://www.info.wien.at). You can e-mail individual inquiries to: inquiries@info.wien.at

All theater tickets can be purchased at the Wien-Ticket-Pavillon, Kärntner Strasse, 1010 Wien (opposite the Staatsoper).

🕐 daily, 10am–7pm

54
Evenings out
THE INSIDER'S FAVORITES

New Year's Day Concert

Tickets for the prestigious New Year's Day Concert are awarded by drawing lots. The winners' names are picked from among all applications received by the first working day of the preceding year. For example, for the concert on January 1, 2002, the closing date will be January 2, 2001. Entries should be sent by letter or telegram to: Wiener Philharmoniker, Bösendorfer Strasse 12, 1010 Wien.

'Wiener Fasching'

The ball season (*Fasching*) opens on the evening of December 31 with the Emperor's Ball and carries on until Shrove Tuesday. Of the vast number of functions, the most famous and fashionable is the *Opernball* at the State Opera. Also worthy of note is the Philharmonic Ball, staged in the magnificent rooms of the Musikverein.

INDEX BY TYPE

There was Gluck, Mozart, Haydn, Beethoven, Schubert; then came
Bruckner, Mahler, Richard Strauss, Schoenberg, Berg, Webern – not to
mention Johann Strauss. This list alone would be sufficient to guarantee
Vienna a place among the great musical capitals of the world. But to these
one must add the Association of the Friends of Viennese Music, the Vienna

After dark

Wiener Staatsoper (1)
Opernring 2, 1010 ☎ (1) 514 442959/2960 ➡ (1) 514 442969

M U1, U2, U4 Karlsplatz **▣** streetcar 1, 2, D, J, etc. **P** **☽** *variable: season
Sep. 1–June 30 ● category A, 120–2,300 schillings; B, 100–2,000 schillings;
C, 50–1,500 schillings; standing room (Stehplatz) 20–30 schillings; standby tickets
(Restkarten) 50 schillings; telephone reservations Mon.–Fri. 8am–6pm; Sat.,
Sun. and public holidays 9am–noon; first Sat. of month 9am–5pm* ▣ ▣ ▣ ▣
@ *http://www.culturall.com (reservations)*

With more than 40 opera productions and some 300 other shows each
season, the Vienna Staatsoper is the world's most prolific repertory
theater. Subscriptions are handed down from one generation to another,
so seats are hard to come by! With a lot of luck, you may get yourself a
seat in the orchestra or one of the 800 standing places – on sale one
hour before the performances from the ticket-office in the foyer.

Musikverein (2)
Bösendorferstrasse 12, 1010 ☎ (1) 505 8190 ➡ (1) 505 8681-94

M U1, U2, U4 Karlsplatz **▣** streetcar 1, 2, D, J **☽** *season: Sep. 1–June 30;
reservations by telephone Mon.–Fri. 9am–7.30pm; Sat. 9am–5pm ● from 50–80
schillings (standing room) to 900 schillings* ▣ ▣

Designed by Theophil Hansen in 1867, the Musikverein plays host to the
prestigious Association of the Friends of Viennese Music. The season is
divided between *Brahmssaal* (chamber music) and *Grosser Saal*
(symphony concerts). It is from this magnificent hall that the annual New
Year's Day concert by the Vienna Philharmonic is televised worldwide.

Wiener Konzerthaus (3)
Lothringerstrasse 20, 1030 ☎ (1) 712 1211 ➡ (1) 712 2872

M U4 Stadtpark **☽** *variable; season: Sep. 1 to June 30; reservations by telephone
Mon.–Fri. 8am–6.30pm; Sat., Sun. and public holidays 10am–1pm and 4–6.30pm*
@ *ticket@konzerthaus.at, http://www.konzerthaus.at*

Vienna's other great musical institution with an international reputation
is to be found only a stone's throw from the Musikverein. Its repertoire
is on the whole more varied and experimental. Every fall there is a
festival of contemporary music, the Wien Modern.

Wiener Volksoper (4)
Währingerstrasse 78, 1090 ☎ (1) 514 442959/2960

M U6 Volksoper **☽** *season: Sep. 1–June 30; reservations by telephone Mon.–Fri.
8am–6pm; Sat., Sun. and public holidays 9am–noon ● 50–99 schillings* ▣ ▣

If there is one place the Viennese like to visit as a family, it is the
Volksoper, the temple of Viennese light opera. Among the repertoire is
Hansel and Gretel, the Viennese operettas of Franz Lehar and Johann
Strauss, and even *The Magic Flute*.

Not forgetting
■ **Wiener Kammeroper (5)** Fleischmarkt 24, 1010, ☎ (1) 513 6072.
Small, intimate hall with interesting programs of chamber music.

Philharmonic Orchestra and the National Opera, directed by famous conductors like Mahler, Karajan, and, more recently, Lorin Maazel, Riccardo Muti and Seiji Ozawa.

Vienna boasts some 50 theaters, including 30 or so independent halls or children's theaters. To these must be added the puppet theater at the Schönbrunn Castle, which delights spectators of all ages with its operas, ballets and fairy tales.

After dark

Burgtheater (6)
Dr-Karl-Lueger-Ring 2, 1010 ☎ (1) 513 1513

streetcar 1, 2, D Rathaus ⊙ *variable: season: Sep.–June; reservations by telephone at least 4 weeks prior to performance, Mon.–Fri. 10am–6pm; Sat., Sun., public holidays, 10am–noon* ● *50–600 schillings*

This temple of Germanic culture ➡ 98 was inaugurated in 1888 with a performance of Franz Grillparzer's *Esther*, since when its staple fare has been German-language classics. The history of the Burgtheater has been dogged by controversies, one of the most notorious occurring in 1988, when Klaus Peymann, who had just been appointed director, staged a performance of Thomas Bernhard's latest drama *Heldenplatz*, dealing with Hitler's annexation of Austria.

Volkstheater (7)
Neustiftgasse 1, 1010 ☎ (1) 524 7263

U2, U3 Volkstheater ⊙ *season: Sep.–June* ● *50–500 schillings*

The Volkstheater was built between 1887 and 1889 on the initiative of a group of Viennese seeking an alternative to the strictly official Burgtheater, thus making well loved classical and contemporary work accessible to a wider public. In July the Volkstheater plays host to *Impuls*, an international festival of dance.

Theater in der Josefstadt (8)
Josefstädterstrasse 24-26, 1080 ☎ (1) 42700/300 ➡ (1) 42700/60

U2 Rathaus J Josefstädterstrasse ⊙ *variable; reservations by telephone at least 14 days prior to performances* ● *50–600 schillings*

The oldest of Vienna's classical stages dates from 1788. The great director Max Reinhardt (co-founder of the world-renowned Salzburg Festival) held sway here from 1923 to 1933, refurbishing the theater and assembling a first-class company, before leaving for self-imposed exile in the States. Today the work of Hofmannsthal and Schnitzler is still performed with tremendous enthusiasm.

Vienna's English Theater (9)
Josefgasse 12, 1080 ☎ (1) 402 1260

U2 Rathaus ⊙ *Mon.–Sat.; season: mid-Sep.–mid-July* ● *180-480 schillings*
Y ⊱ Stadiongasse

Founded in 1963 by the Austrian Franz Schafranek and his American actress-wife Ruth Brinkmann, the company took up permanent residence here in 1974. Originally conceived as a theater for English-speaking tourists, it soon developed an annual program of productions thanks to an enthusiastic reception by the Viennese public. Grace Kelly, Jeanne Moreau, Joan Fontaine, Anthony Quinn, Vittorio Gassmann and Jean-Louis Barrault are among the great actors who have trodden its boards.

Not forgetting

■ **Kammerspiele (10)** Rotenturmstrasse 20, 1010 U3, U4, Schwedenplatz. *Small theater specializing in controversial productions; Schnitzler's erotic masterpiece La Ronde caused a scandal when first performed here in 1921.*

Austria's status as one of the world's great musical centers would have been incomplete without its operettas and musical comedies. Between the wars, Vienna could count some 25 cabarets tucked away in cellars. Today there is a clear resurgence of this genre, with a good 10 cabarets in various parts of the city.

After dark

Raimundtheater (11)
Wallgasse 18, 1060 ☎ (1) 5997727

🅼 *U6 Gumpendorferstr.* 🕔 *variable; box office 10am–7pm, closed July–Aug*
● *130–1,300 schillings; telephone reservations to Wien-Ticket ☎ (1) 58885*
➡ *(1) 588 3033* 🔲 ♿

The name derives from the great dramatist Ferdinand Raimund (1790–1836) whose work was the inspiration for the golden age of Viennese popular theater. After 1948, under the then director Rudolf Marik, the Raimundtheater became one of the showcases of musical comedy: *Grease*, *The Lady and the Tramp* plus *Kiss of the Spider-Woman* (*The Vampires' Ball*) – a 1997 Roman Polanski production with music by Jim Steinman – have all been performed here.

Theater an der Wien (12)
Linke Wienzeile 6, 1060 ☎ (1) 588 30310/315

🅼 *U2, U4 Karlsplatz* ● *300–1300 schillings* 🔲 ♿

The impresario Emanuel Schikaneder opened this theater in 1801 to replace the Theater auf der Wieden which, ten years before, had witnessed the triumphant first night of Mozart's *The Magic Flute*. The theater also staged the premieres of Beethoven's Fidelio (1805) and Johann Strauss's *Die Fledermaus* (1874). The Theater an der Wien still produces smash-hit musical comedies – 1.27 million spectators from all over the globe traveled to see *Elisabeth* between 1993 and 1998 – but it is displaying a tendency to revert to its original intention by presenting operas and operettas at festivals such as the Wiener Festwochen (June) and the Klangbogen (July–August).

Ronacher (13)
Seilerstätte 9, 1010 ☎ (1) 51411

🔳 *streetcar 1, 2 Parkring* 🕔 *10am–7pm reservations by telephone to Wien-Ticket ☎ (1) 58885* ➡ *(1) 588 3033* ● *variable* 🔲 ♿

Between 1887 and 1888, the impresario Anton Ronacher transformed the Wiener Stadttheater into a variety house. The financial difficulties which rapidly confronted him obliged him to retire from the project in 1890. From then on the theater staged shows of every kind: operettas, revues, drama, acrobats, magicians… After restoration in the early 1990s, the Ronacher has reopened with an eclectic program reflecting the vagaries of its financial situation. But watch the billboards: pleasant surprises occur.

Kulisse (14)
Rosensteingasse 39, 1170 ☎ (1) 485 3870

🔳 *J, 44 J.-N.-Berger-Platz* 🕔 *performances 8pm, box office 6pm–1am; Sep. 1–June 30; closed July–Aug* ● *180–220 schillings* @ *http://www.kulisse.at*

Every evening, the Kulisse stages first-rate shows starring famous cabaret comedians. The atmosphere is great, but to really understand *Wiener Schmäh*, the Viennese sense of humor, you need to know the dialect, so audiences tend to be confined to German-speakers. After the show, you can wine and dine at the *Beisl*, a tavern in the purest local traditions.

Not forgetting

■ **Simpl (15)** Wollzeile 36, 1010 ☎ (1) 512 4732. *Typically Viennese cabaret.*

Vienna is certainly not a great jazz capital, but there are a few good venues where fans can indulge their passion. Note too that the Wiener Konzerthaus ➡ 66 has occasional jazz programs, and every year the city organizes the Fest Wien jazz festival, frequently advertised on a grand scale with much alluring publicity.

After dark

Jazzland (16)
Franz Joseph Kai 29, 1010 ☎ (1) 533 2575

Ⓜ *U1, U4 Schwedenplatz* Ⓞ *Mon.–Sat.; concerts start 9pm* ● *variable*

Here is an authentic jazz club installed in a medieval cellar. Every evening they revive the standards of blues and boogie, folk, swing, traditional and modern jazz. Live music usually from around 9pm. Food and drink available before, during and after the show.

Krah Krah (17)
Rabensteig 8, 1010 ☎ (1) 533 8193

Ⓜ *U1, U4 Schwedenplatz* Ⓞ *Mon.–Sat. 11–2am; Sun. and public holidays 11–1am* ● *admission free*

Jazz-lovers will enjoy brunching or lunching here on Sundays when the bar of the Krah Krah – in the 'Bermuda Triangle area' – plays host to a live group from 11.30am to 3pm. The rest of the time this is a lively tavern offering one of the best choices of beers in the capital.

Tunnel (18)
Florianigasse 39, 1080 ☎ (1) 405 3465

▦ *5 , J, bus 13 A* Ⓞ *9–2am, shows start 9pm* ● *variable*

Popular with students for its low prices, the Tunnel has a concert room in the basement reserved mainly for jazz groups. From time to time they make a foray into blues, rock or bossa nova. On Sunday evenings admission is free for 'Jazz Live', starting at 8pm.

Reigen (19)
Hadikgasse 62, 1140 ☎ (1) 894 0094

Ⓜ *U4 Hietzing* Ⓞ *bar, restaurant, 6pm–4am; shows start 9pm* ● *150 schillings* @ *http://www.onstage.at/reigen*

You can combine an evening out with a visit to the Schönbrunn castle. The Reigen has jazz concerts virtually every day, with a preference for Latin-American rhythms. On Saturdays there is a salsa evening.

Miles Smiles (20)
Langegasse 51, 1080 ☎ (1) 405 9517

Ⓜ *U2 Rathaus* ▦ *J Lederergasse, 13A Lederergasse* Ⓞ *Sun.–Thu. 8pm–2am; Fri., Sat. 8pm–4am* ● *about 100–150 schillings for live evenings*

Jazz fans will discover a warm welcome here. You can grab a bite to eat and a drink while listening to jazz from the 1950s onward. Two or three concerts every month.

Not forgetting

■ **Porgy & Bess (21)** *One of the capital's best jazz venues, closed until the fall of 2000 for renovations, though sessions are still staged outside the city center on Wednesday evenings at the Meierei im Stadtpark ➡ 74 and at the Radio Kultur Haus,* Argentinierstrasse 30a, 1040 ☎ (1) 501 0118067 ■ **Papa's Tapas (22)** Schwarzenbergplatz 10, 1040 ☎ (1) 505 0311 *Blues concerts every day except Sun. (July–Aug., Thu.–Sat. only).*

Synonymous with the classics in the popular mind, Vienna nevertheless plays host to music of every sort.

It's not just waltz rhythm that sets the Viennese dancing; after dark, the city comes alive to the throbbing beat of electronic music. Clubs contend to hire the best and trendiest DJs. Some, Vienna-born and graduates of the city's night clubs, have made their names well beyond the frontiers of Austria: Kruder, Dorfmeister, Pulsinger, Tunakam, to name a few.

After dark

Flex (23)
Donaukanal/Augartenbrücke, 1010 ☎ (1) 533 7525

Ⓜ U2, U4 Schottenring 🚋 1, 2 Schottenring ● 100 schillings approximately

A trendy club occupying an old warehouse on the bank of the Donaukanal, Flex organizes theme evenings with bands and individual performers from differing musical worlds. One of the coolest scenes for electronic music. Things usually get going after 11pm.

Pl Disco (24)
Rotgasse 9, 1010 ☎ (1) 535 9995

Ⓜ U3, U4 Schwedenplatz 🚋 1, 2 Schwedenplatz

On the edge of the 'Bermuda Triangle' – the central district where young Viennese go to drown their cares on Saturday evenings. Absolutely *the* disco for techno freaks.

Meierei im Stadtpark (25)
Am Heumarkt 2A, 1030 ☎ (1) 714 6159

🕐 Wed.–Sat ● about 100 schillings

You will find this club in an offbeat setting: a quaint, late 19th-century edifice in the middle of the Stadtpark (municipal park). Open Wednesdays–Saturdays: two dance floors reverberating to the sound of house and garage.

Volksgarten Disco (26)
Burgring 1, 1010 ☎ (1) 533 0518

🚋 1, 2, D Dr-Karl-Renner-Ring 🕐 Thu., Fri., Sat. and every 1st, 3rd and 5th Wed. of month, from 10 or 11pm ● about 100 schillings @ http://www.volksgarten.at

Opposite the Hofburg Imperial Palace, on the edge of the Volksgarten, this is where Vienna's students hang out and dance to house, techno, hip hop, soul, reggae… Theme evenings are the rule.

Titanic (27)
Theobaldgasse 11, 1060 ☎ (1) 587 4758

Ⓜ U2 Babenbergerstrasse 🕐 Thu.–Sat. from 9.30pm ● admission free

There are two dance floors in the basement, one specializing in hip hop, the other mainly devoted to 1980s revival. There is a ground-floor restaurant open from Tuesday to Saturday.

U4 (28)
Schönbrunnerstrasse 222, 1120

Ⓜ U4 Meidlinger Hauptstrasse 🕐 10pm–5am ● 60–100 schillings

A classic among Vienna's discos. Two dance halls with a wide variety of music.

Not forgetting

■ **WUK (29)** Werkstätten und Kulturhaus, Währingerstrasse 59, 1090 ☎ (1) 40121/0. *Independent cultural center. Regularly stages first-rate musical evenings.* @ http://www.wuk.at.

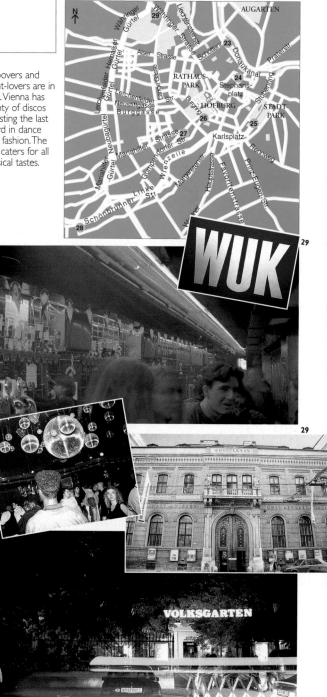

Groovers and night-lovers are in luck. Vienna has plenty of discos boasting the last word in dance and fashion. The city caters for all musical tastes.

The center of gravity of Vienna's trendy nightlife has recently shifted to the Gürtel, the peripheral road encircling the city. This former sleazy, rundown area is now in the throes of a full-scale renovation; some excellent bars with a burgeoning clientele have sprung up under the arches of the elevated railroad (U6) designed by Otto Wagner at the

After dark

Blue Box (30)
Richtergasse 8, 1070 ☎ (1) 523 2682

Ⓜ U3, Neubaugasse Ⓢ Tue.–Sun. 10–2am; Mon. 6pm–2am ● admission free

The DJ keeps the music discreet; the club's aim is to provide a place where you can come and chat with friends.

B 72 (31)
Hernalsergürtel, U-Bahnbögen 72/73, 1080 ☎ (1) 409 2128

Ⓜ U6, Alserstrasse Ⓢ 8pm–4am ● variable (admission free until 10pm)

This is a new scene, encapsulated under the red brick arches of the elevated railroad, with a different DJ each evening. Some nights are theme nights: Friday until 6am is tempo night, for instance. There's a dance floor if you feel the urge…

Chelsea (32)
Lerchenfeldergürtel, U-Bahnbögen 29/31, 1080 ☎ (1) 407 9309

Ⓜ U6 Josefstädterstrasse Ⓢ 8pm–4am ● variable @ chelsea@silverserver.co.at http://www.chelsea.co.at/chelsea/

An underground scene dating from 1986, predominantly pop. A different DJ every night. The Chelsea does more than hire entertainers or stage good gigs by local or international bands; it also stamps its personality on the music world by producing a fanzine four times a year. Cider, scotch and Irish beer flow when they are showing British or Austrian football on the big-screen TVs.

Rhiz (33)
Lerchenfeldergürtel, U-Bahnbögen 29/31, 1080 ☎ (1) 409 2505

Ⓜ U6 Josefstädterstrasse Ⓢ 6pm–4am ● 100 schillings @ http://www.rhiz.org

New electronic scene. Live performer with a battery of equipment virtually every night from 8pm; once the audience is warmed up, the DJ takes over.

Kunsthalle Café (34)
Treitlstrasse 2, 1040 ☎ (1) 586 9864

Ⓜ U2, U4 Karlsplatz Ⓢ 10–2am ● variable

Easy to find, just behind the Kunsthalle, the big yellow building bang in the middle of the Karlsplatz, not far from the Secession Building. A different DJ each evening from 10pm. Terrace open in summer.

Not forgetting

■ **Volksgarten-Pavillon (35)** Volksgarten, 1010. The place to discover Vienna's youth and beauty from April to September, every Tuesday, Wednesday and Sunday from 9pm. Lively sounds; good DJs. Admission to pavilion terraces free.

start of the 20th century.

Dozens of bars have sprung up in places until recently shunned by tourists. Today, these areas are rapidly discovering a new existence as the centers of Vienna's booming clubland.

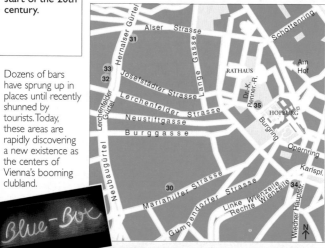

Bars with live music

Blue-Bar

30

31

34

It is hard to advise on a choice of bars; it depends on your taste – and your mood – whether you want a quiet retreat or somewhere really switched-on. But here are a few places that may appeal to you. There is one area you really must explore if you are seeking authentic wine bars: the Schönlaterngasse ➡ 90.

After dark

Schultz (36)
Siebensterngasse 31, 1070 Wien ☎ (1) 522 9120

🔲 49 ◷ Mon.–Sat. 9–2am; Sun. 5pm–2am @ schultz@magnet.at

A cocktail bar opened in 1996: one of the 'in' places at aperitif time. Take a peep at its designer décor through the glass bay windows. The initial impression of chilliness is deceptive; the atmosphere is friendly and the choice of drinks first-class.

Stein (37)
Währingerstrasse 6, 1090 ☎ (1) 319 7241

Ⓜ U2, U4 Schottentor ◷ 8–1am @ http://www.cafe-stein.co.at-cafe-stein

Vienna's first cybercafé. Internet freaks love to meet and be seen here. But don't come along to chat; the decibel level makes it hard going! You can still have a great evening out, with good, funky music… If you must have peace and quiet, try the terrace in the afternoon.

Plutzer Bräu (38)
Schrankgasse 2, 1070 ☎ (1) 526 1215

Ⓜ U2, U3 Volkstheater 🔲 48A ◷ 11.30–2am

This is a popular place for students: a large tavern in the very heart of Spittelberg ➡ 36. Some good house beers, tasty canapés and sandwiches, or, more traditionally, spareribs. Great atmosphere.

Santo Spirito (39)
Kumpfgasse 7, 1010 ☎ (1) 512 9998

Ⓜ U3 Stubento ◷ 11–2am; Sat. 11–3am; Sun. 10–2am

For lovers of classical music – Baroque in particular – a welcoming bar open every evening long after the shows close. But reserve a table in advance if you want dinner: the place is very popular.

Not forgetting

■ **MAK Café (40)** Stubenring 3/5 ☎ (1) 714 0121 Ⓜ U3 Stubentor ◷ 10am–2am, closed Mon. *The café of the Museum of Applied Arts is also a restaurant. The main room has a curious coffered ceiling, but the rest of the décor is modernist. Two portholes pierced in one of the walls give an unusual view right into the museum. There is a pleasant terrace for the summer between two of the museum buildings.*
■ **Die Wäscherei (41)** Albertgasse 49, 1080 ☎ (1) 409 237511. *Recently opened; a modern, friendly establishment serving an excellent Weiss Bier (a type of light ale) brewed in Salzburg.*
■ **Europa (42)** Zollergasse 8 ☎ (1) 526 3383. *Night-owls will be relieved: there really are bars in Vienna which stay open very late: the Europa, for example, which doesn't close until 5am.*

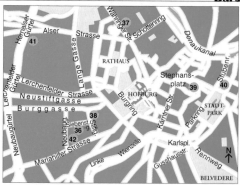

Vienna has enjoyed a long-standing love affair with its cafés. Today, cybercafés, taverns, avant-garde establishments and traditional bars rub shoulders.

The Viennese café is an institution; people don't just stop by, they virtually take up residence. They come to chat, put the world to rights, study the international press, take a siesta — and, incidentally, drink coffee or eat a cake. Intellectuals, artists, politicians… all have their *Stammtisch* (special table) or their 'regular day'.

After dark

Café Central (43)
Herrengasse 14, 1010 ☎ (1) 533 3763

M *U3 Herrengasse* ○ *8am–8pm (summer), 8am–10pm (winter); closed Sun. and public holidays; live music 4pm–7pm*

One of the most distinguished and cosmopolitan of Vienna's cafés, occupying Heinrich Ferstel's neo-Renaissance palace. More popular with tourists than with the Viennese, but still a must for its opulent décor and its choice of patisseries.

Café Hawelka (44)
Dorotheergasse 6, 1010 ☎ (1) 512 8230

M *U1, U3 Stephansplatz* ○ *Tue.–Sat. 8–2am; Sun. and public holidays 10–2am; closed Mon.*

The Hawelka family have owned this café for 60 years, and delight in recalling the time when artists came here to sell their canvases in exchange for a bowl of soup or a portion of bread. Times have moved on, but the atmosphere remains as cordial as ever. In any case, don't miss the tasty *Buchtein*, small cakes filled with a type of plum jam which Frau Hawelka assiduously prepares herself!

Café Bräunerhof (45)
Stallburggasse 2, 1010 ☎ (1) 512 3893

M *U1, U3 Stephansplatz* ○ *Mon.–Fri. 7.30am–8.30pm; Sat., Sun. and public holidays 10am–6pm*

The dramatist Thomas Bernhard had his *Stammtisch* (special table) in this very typical Viennese café. On Saturdays, Sundays and public holidays, from 4pm to 6pm, a delightful piano trio plays Viennese music.

Café Griensteidl (46)
Michaelerplatz 2, 1010 ☎ (1) 535 2692/93

M *U3 Herrengasse* ○ *8am–midnight*

Established in 1847 by the pharmacist Heinrich Griensteidl, the Griensteidl became the haunt of numerous Austrian artists and intellectuals — Hofmannsthal, Schnitzler, Kraus, Wolf, Schoenberg — only to close on the death of its proprietor in 1897. Happily, it reopened its doors in 1990, and became once more a grand Viennese institution.

Café Sperl (47)
Gumpendorferstrasse 11, 1060 ☎ (1) 586 4158

M *U2 Gumpendorferstrasse* ○ *Mon.–Sat. 7am–11pm; Sun. and public holidays 3pm–11pm; closed Sun. and public holidays in July and Aug.*

One of those old Viennese cafés where time seems to have stopped, so serene and peaceful is the atmosphere. Fans of French billiards can satisfy their addiction at the three tables.

Not forgetting

■ **Café Prückel (48)** Stubenring 24, 1010 ☎ (1) 512 6115 ○ 9am–10pm
■ **Café Diglas (49)** Wollzeile 10, 1010 ☎ (1) 512 5765/0 ○ 7am–midnight
■ **Café Landtmann (50)** Dr-Karl-Lueger-Ring 1010 ☎ (1) 532 0621

43

44

50

47

45

The extraordinary variety of Viennese patisseries recalls the luxury of the Imperial Household. When the Habsburgs ruled much of Europe, they sent for master flan-makers from Bohemia and specialists in caramels and icing from the court of Burgundy, where they had relations. They even borrowed their famous strudel from the Turks, via the Hungarians.

After dark

Demel (51)
Kohlmarkt 14, 1010 ☎ (1) 535 1717/39

Ⓜ *U1, U3 Stephansplatz* 🕙 *10am–7pm* ▭ ▣ ♿ ✖

Demel is considered by Viennese to be the home of patisserie. If Viennese *Konditoreien* live up to their reputation as the world's best, then Demel must be the finest patisserie in existence. The interior décor – all velvet and gilding, a perfect incarnation of late 19th-century Vienna – is matched by the exemplary service, worthy of a great establishment. Demel's delights include cunning hors d'oeuvre; sweets with seductive names like Gateau Anna, Fragility, *crème du jour*; candies and chocolates in gift boxes as exquisite as jewel cases and based on designs by leading Jugendstil figures, and *Veilchenbonbon* – the cachous adored by the Empress Sissi. The terrace overlooks the Kohlmarkt, Vienna's most elegant commercial thoroughfare. This is the place to sit in fine weather; let time wash over you as you watch the ebb and flow of passers-by in the shadow of the Michaelertor dome, at the entrance to the Hofburg.

Oberlaaer Stadthaus (52)
Neuer Markt 16, 1010 ☎ (1) 513 2936

Ⓜ *U1, U3 Stephansplatz* 🕙 *Mon.–Fri. 8am–7pm; Sat., Sun. and public holidays 8am–10pm; summer: daily 8am–10pm* ▭ ▣ ▣ ▣ ✖

This *Konditorei* prepares gateaux as light as a feather, delicious-smelling *petits fours* to accompany coffee, plus salads and other dishes for a quick lunch. With a pleasant view over the Donnerbrunnen, the terrace offers a moment of relaxation after tramping around the city. Don't leave Vienna without one of Oberlaaer's specialties: the gift wrappings are as gorgeous as the contents are delicious. ★ A tip: the *Faschingskrapfen* (doughnuts filled with apricot jam) are rated the best in Vienna.

Gerstner (53)
Kärntnerstrasse 21/23, 1010 ☎ (1) 512 6863

Ⓜ *U1, U3 Stephansplatz* 🕙 *Mon.–Sat. 9am–10pm; Sun. 10am–10pm* ▭ ▣
▣ ✖

A city-center *Konditorei* with a restaurant service at midday and plenty of variety: the *Gassenlokal* (bar-restaurant) on the ground floor, a first-floor restaurant with a view over the Kärtner Strasse, and a large terrace. Gerstner has certainly found how to keep the children amused: they are invited to make their own little marzipan candies.

Sluka (54)
Rathausplatz 8, 1010 ☎ (1) 405 7172

Ⓜ *U2 Rathaus* 🕙 *Mon.–Fri. 8am–7pm; Sat. 8am–5.30pm* ▣ ▣ ▣ ✖

Next door to the Rathaus or City Hall, whence the name of a nut cake – *Bürgermeister* or 'Mayor's Cake' – which has made the Sluka famous. All the classic Viennese patisseries, plus a range of *petits fours* and sandwiches. The tiered wedding-cakes are very impressive-looking feats of engineering. In summer, you'll enjoy the terrace under the arches.

Konditorei
Sluka

54

Rathaus-platz
54
Dr.-K.-Renner-R.
Herrengasse
Kohlmkt
Graben
Stephans-platz
51
Volkstheater
Burgring
HOFBURG
Parkring
52
Kärntner Strasse
53
Museumsplatz
BURG-GARTEN
Opernring
N

52

51

52

53

54

51

What to see

The Wien Karte (Vienna Card)

➥ 12–13 ● *210 schillings*
The Wien Karte is valid for travel on all forms of transport for three days, as well as entitling you to reduced entry fees to certain public buildings. Obtainable at information centers; also by telephone – have your credit card details ready.
☎ (1) 798 4400-28.

Around the Ring

The Ring is the impressive peripheral road constructed in the 19th century around Vienna's historic center and on the site of the former fortifications. Most of the city's major monuments are located on this circuit. You can make the round trip on foot or by streetcar. But there's another way — by horse-drawn carriage. Shorter trips (20 mins) cost 500 schillings, the 40-minute version is 800 schillings.

72
Sights
THE INSIDER'S FAVORITES

Vienna's museums and galleries

Note that all major public buildings are closed on Mondays. A list of museums, etc., together with other information, can be found on the Internet. @ www.nhm.wien.ac.at/bundesmuseen

INDEX BY TYPE

Europe's fourth largest city by 1910, Vienna had become a magnet for ethnic groups from all over an empire covering some 270,000 square miles. After two World Wars, the capital underwent periods of severe crisis. Now recovered from its wounds, Vienna has regained the happy atmosphere which contributes so much to its charm.

What to see

True Europeans

Vienna has been successively the village home of a Slavic tribe, a Roman stronghold on the Danube frontier and the glittering capital of the Habsburg monarchy – a dynasty which, at the head of an empire speaking seven languages, ruled Austria for over six centuries and twice saw the city besieged by the Turks. Vienna was, and still is, the meeting-point of several worlds: Germanic, Slav, Balkan and Mediterranean. It is the cosmopolitan heart of a country which, while remaining faithful to its traditions, elected in 1995 to join the European Union. As such, it is more than a treasure-house of the past; very much alive and unlikely to fossilize, Vienna is a city on a human scale.

A cultural capital

'The streets of Vienna are paved with culture as streets in other cities are with asphalt.' This, not without justification, is how Karl Kraus describes a city containing one of the world's richest art galleries (the Kunsthistorisches Museum), the largest collection of drawings and engravings (the Albertina), not to mention manuscripts of inestimable value (the Nationalbibliotek). Is that all? Hardly! The name of Vienna is also inextricably linked with music. At the Staatsoper, the Musikverein or the Konzerthaus – homes of the Singakademie, the Singverein and the Philharmonie – nightly homage is paid to the city's famous composers: Haydn, Mozart, Schubert, Mahler, Schoenberg. Each year the whirling Viennese balls and the intoxication of Strauss's waltzes attract millions of visitors dreaming of following in the steps of the Empress Sissi and reliving the brilliant era of the Habsburgs. No less fertile in novelists and playwrights, Vienna can boast Schnitzler, Hofmannsthal and Bernhard, whose prestigious works are performed regularly at the Burgtheater. On the street fronts, Jugendstil architecture rubs shoulders with Baroque masterpieces, neoclassical palaces and daring contemporary experiments. But also part of Viennese culture is that dialect – soft as a caress – the multiracial population, a widely diverse cuisine and those legendary cafés.

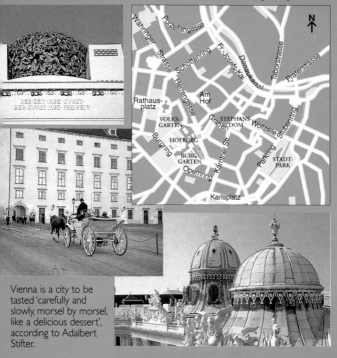

Vienna is a city to be tasted 'carefully and slowly, morsel by morsel, like a delicious dessert', according to Adalbert Stifter.

A 'green' city

To the west is the Weinerwald with its majestic beech woods; eastward, the Danube flows through the green parkland of the Prater whose horizons fade into the Hungarian and Slovakian plains. South of the city, beneath the gaze of nearby Alpine peaks, sprawl the unspoilt woodlands of the Lobau where the river meanders among its labyrinth of backwaters. Nature is never far from the thoughts of the Viennese, forming an integral part of their lives. Her changing rhythms govern and inspire the work of artists and musicians – Beethoven took daily walks through the Nussdorf vines, the Danube and the Vienna Woods haunt the music of Strauss, poplars and beeches recur in the paintings of Klimt. The sculptor Fritz Wotruba writes: 'I dream of a sculpture where the landscape, the architecture and the city dissolve into a single work of art.' Hundertwassser visualizes houses in all the colors of a spring landscape, turning his back on straight lines which 'are non-existent in Nature'. Vienna's identity has evolved, in fact, through striking a healthy balance with its natural surroundings.

A taste for living

The daily chores over, time for social life and relaxation. The people of Vienna love to stroll in the spacious city parks, to sit whiling away the hours in conversation in those big, timeless cafés. Or they go further afield to the taverns *(Heurigen)* scattered around the slopes, where you will find them drinking a glass of white wine to the plaintive and melancholy strains of violins and the accordion. They throng the theaters and concert halls, as well as cabarets echoing to the laughter inspired by *Schmäh*, Vienna's unique sense of humor. They gather on the Rathausplatz, where every season brings its own joys: the circus in the fall, a Christmas market and ice-skating in winter, and in summer a highly popular music festival. Between the New Year celebrations and Shrovetide is the season for balls and galas.

In the area
- Where to stay: ➡ 24 ➡ 28
- Where to eat: ➡ 42 ➡ 44
- After dark: ➡ 70 ➡ 78 ➡ 80 ➡ 82
- Where to shop: ➡ 136 ➡ 140

What to see

Stephansdom (1)
Stephansplatz, 1010 ☎ (1) 515 52-3767

M U1, U3 Stephansplatz ⊙ 6am–10pm; Fri. 7am–10pm ● Admission free
Cathedral Mon.–Sat. 10.30am and 3pm, Sun. and public holidays 3pm;
Catacombs Mon.–Sat. 10–11.30am, 1.30–4.30pm, every 30 mins., Sun. and
public holidays, afternoons only ● 40 schillings; **Steffl Tower** 9am–5.30pm
● 30 schillings; **Pummerin Tower** 9am–5.30pm ● 40 schillings

The cathedral spire, familiarly known as the Steffl by the Viennese, has,
over the centuries, become the city's symbol. St Stephen's Cathedral
replaced a Romanesque basilica erected in the 12th century and
reconstructed in the 13th. The addition in 1556 of a cupola to the
unfinished north tower was the crowning glory of 200 years' work. The
only surviving parts of the Romanesque building are the Riesentor
(Giants' Gateway) and the twin Towers of the Pagans. During the
bombing of 1945, the wonderful diamond-patterned roof collapsed in a
sea of flames and, like the nave, had to be rebuilt piece by piece. Inside,
the eye is unfailingly drawn to the pulpit in the central aisle of the nave,
a masterpiece of flamboyant Gothic, and a *tour de force* of the
goldsmith's art by its creator Anton Pilgram, who depicted himself
peering out from under the steps. Don't overlook the superb rose
windows and numerous statues (also Gothic). In the choir, look for the
retable, and the tomb of Rudolph IV – the cathedral's traditional founder
– in the north apse; the resting place of Frederick III can be found
opposite, in the south apse. Those brave souls who climb the 343 steps
of the Steffl will be rewarded with a breathtaking view. Others will have
to be content with the north tower.

Figarohaus (2)
Domgasse 5, 1010 ☎ (1) 513 6294

M U1, U3, Stephansplatz ⊙ 9am–6pm, closed Mon., Jan. 1, May 1 and Dec. 25
● Adults 25 schillings, concessions 10 schillings.

It was in this 17th-century house that Mozart lived between 1784 and
1787 and composed, among other works, *The Marriage of Figaro*, the first
performance of which took place on May 1, 1786 at the Hofburg. Today
the building houses a Mozart museum.

Franziskanerkirche (3)
Franziskanerplatz 4, 1010

M U1, U3, Stephansplatz ; U3 Stubentor ; U4 Stadtpark

Most of the appeal of the Franziskanerplatz derives from the Moses
Fountain (1798), and the Franciscan church (1603–11) which gives the
square its name. The façade of the Franziskanerkirche – in the Renaissance
style of southern Germany – is almost unique in Vienna. The Baroque
interior boasts an ornate high altar by Andrea Pozzo.

Not forgetting
■**Schatzkammer des Deutschen Ordens (4)** Singerstrasse 7, 1010
☎ (1) 533 7931 M U3 Stephansplatz. *Dissolved by Napoleon in 1809, the
Order of Teutonic Knights was resurrected in Vienna, its original home since the
1300s. The Treasury is in the House of the Teutonic Order.*

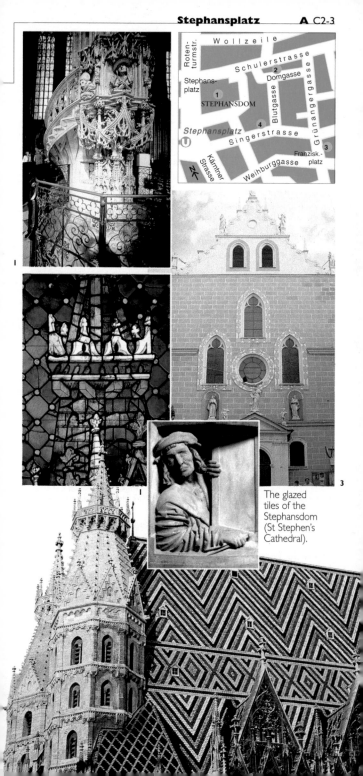

The glazed tiles of the Stephansdom (St Stephen's Cathedral).

In the area

🔲 **Where to stay:** ➡ 30
🔲 **Where to eat:** ➡ 42 ➡ 44
🔲 **After dark:** ➡ 66 ➡ 70 ➡ 78 ➡ 80
🔲 **Where to shop:** ➡ 140 ➡ 148–149

▶ What to see

Zwölf Apostelkeller (5)
Sonnenflesgasse 3, 1010 ☎ (01) 512 6777

Ⓜ U3, U1 Stephansplatz 🕐 4.30pm–midnight

There is a restaurant in the massive brick vaults, but they are worth a visit in themselves, with their powerful evocation of 14th- and 15th-century Vienna.

Schönlaterngasse (6)
Schönlaterngasse, 1010

This is a delightful little street retaining a medieval atmosphere. No. 6 sports a copy of the 'beautiful lantern' referred to in its name. Opposite, a sandstone beast-sculpture, very little restored, announces no. 7, the Basiliskenhaus, as it was already called in the 12th century. It is said to depict the basilisk which the owner of the house, a baker, got rid of by a clever ploy. The fabulous creature, whose looks were reputed to kill, had set up home in the well and poisoned it with its breath. The baker had the idea of climbing down with a mirror, and when the basilisk looked at its reflection, it was turned to stone. Just before the Basiliskenhaus is a covered passageway. This leads to a courtyard surrounded by a group of 17th- and 18th-century buildings, including the Bernhardskapelle (St Bernard's Chapel), which belonged to the monastery of Heilingenskreuz.

Jesuitenkirche/Universitätskirche (7)
Dr-Ignaz-Seipel-Platz 1, 1010

The church, though a Jesuit construction (1627–31), incorporated to perfection the architectural principles of the Counter-Reformation. The relative austerity of its flat façade – relieved nevertheless by the two bell towers with their lanterns – contrasts with the interior, which was drastically altered in the following century. The ceiling frescos (1705) are the work of Baroque artist Andrea Pozzo, the great Italian master of trompe l'oeil.

Alte Universität (8)
Dr.-Ignaz-Seipel-Platz 1, 1010

The sworn enemy of Protestantism, Ferdinand II gave his backing to the Jesuits, who were to run the University of Vienna until the reforms introduced by Maria Theresa in 1761. The years 1623–7 had witnessed the rise of a plain and severe group of buildings; from 1753 to 1755 a large Baroque-style edifice began to take shape under the direction of a French architect.

Dominikanerkirche (9)
Postgasse 4, 1010

In the 13th century, on the Postgasse, the Dominicans founded a monastery, and a church which has been rebuilt several times. The present Baroque version, modeled on originals in Rome, dates from 1631 to 1634.

Not forgetting

■ **Akademie der Wissenschaft (10)** Dr.-Ignaz-Seipel-Platz 2, 1010
The Academy of Sciences acquired this large university building in 1883.

The Jesuit and Dominican churches, both inside and out, conform closely to the canons of Baroque architecture.

In the area
■ **Where to stay:** ➡ 24 ➡ 26
■ **Where to eat:** ➡ 42 ➡ 46
■ **After dark:** ➡ 74 ➡ 80 ➡ 82
■ **Where to shop:** ➡ 138–139 ➡ 142 ➡ 144 ➡ 148–149

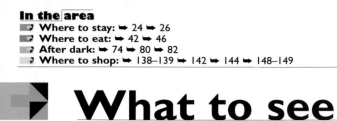

What to see

Graben (11)
Graben, 1010

When *Vindobona* was a mere Roman outpost on the Danube frontier, this was a defensive ditch (*Graben*). Like the other one guarding the eastern approach, it was filled in in 1255 when Vienna overflowed its original boundaries. The wide avenue, closed to traffic, is one of the city's most elegant thoroughfares and a paradise for window-shoppers. Among the apartment buildings on either side, notice the neoclassical façade of no. 21 (1835–8) which was Austria's first savings bank. No. 16, the Ankerhaus (Anchor House), was designed by the mastermind of the 'Secessionist' transition from Historicism to the form of Art Nouveau known as Jugendstil: Otto Wagner. By its juxtaposition of different materials, the building illustrates his passionate interest in new construction mediums and the use of metal. In the center of the Graben, between the fountains of Saint Leopold and Saint Joseph, rises the Plague Column. This huge votive offering, commissioned by the emperor Leopold I on the ending of the scourge which decimated Vienna in 1679, provided employment for numerous Austrian and Italian artists. At the meeting of the Graben and the Stephansplatz, you will most likely be surprised to come across a large wooden stump studded with nails. This is the Stock im Eisen; journeyman blacksmiths came and planted nails in it for luck.

Peterskirche (12)
Petersplatz, 1010

This pure expression of Baroque dates from the 18th century and was built on the site of one of Vienna's oldest churches. Standing back from the Graben, the Peterskirche surges upward in a series of curves and counter-curves under its oval dome, through which light floods the interior. Don't miss the *Assumption* frescos (by Michael Rottmayr, in the cupola), and, opposite the pulpit, the gilded carving of the martyrdom of Saint John Nepomuk, the patron saint of Bohemia, who was drowned in 1393 for refusing to reveal the queen's confessional secrets to Wenceslas IV.

Michaeler Platz (13)
Michaeler Platz, 1010

Recently discovered remains indicate Roman occupation of the site. The square is dominated by the Michaeltor (St Michael's Gate), the principal entrance to the Imperial Palace, with its superb ironwork. Opposite is no. 13, a house (1910) which belonged to Adolf Loos, one of the chief Secessionist artists. The sight of this 'house with no eyebrows', as contemporary Viennese satirized it, is said to have irritated the emperor so much that he had all the curtains of the palace closed, and avoided using the Michaeltor. St Michael's is a loose blend of styles. Before entering, note the polychrome relief of the Mount of Olives in a passage along the church wall. Inside, there is the stone monument, in Renaissance style, of Georg von Liechtenstein, and an impressive high altar.

Not forgetting

■ **Naglergasse (14)**, 1010. *This peaceful little backwater off the Graben has preserved an old-world charm with fine 17th- and 18th-century house-fronts in different colors. Here time has stood still – as in the Kurrentgasse, where tourists can still ride in a fiaker (trap), and which leads to the Judenplatz.*

11

12

13

13

13

▶ What to see

Synagogue (15)
Seittenstettengasse 4, 1010

Vienna's Jewish community, already sizeable in the Middle Ages, had grown to 200,000 by the interwar period. Though expelled from the city center during the Hussite wars of the 15th century, Jews had greater freedom under the Habsburgs. By the Edict of Tolerance (1781), Joseph II opened the way to total emancipation, finally achieved in 1867; he recognized the right of non-Catholics to practice their own religions – in a discreet manner. This explains the unobtrusive siting of the Great Synagogue and its escape from the destruction of *Kristallnacht,* a massive pogrom against Jews throughout Hitler's Reich.

Ruprechtskirche (16)
Seitenstettengasse 5, 1010

This is the French parish, and boasts the oldest church in Vienna. According to tradition, the little building dedicated to Saint Rupert, Bishop of Worms and later Salzburg, was founded in 740. Altered over the centuries, it has preserved its Romanesque nave as well as the base of the 11th-century bell tower. One of the stained-glass windows in the chancel dates from the 13th century. The Black Virgin above the altar protected the Viennese from the Turks and the Plague.

Hoher Markt (17)
Hoher Markt, 1010

The Old Market occupies the site of the Roman forum, traces of which have been excavated; access through no. 3. In the Middle Ages, the Hoher Markt was also used for public hangings. It was badly damaged during World War Two, but the Fountain of the Virgin's Wedding survives in the center, and, on one side, the Ankeruhr (Anchor Clock) designed by Franz von Matsch in 1913. Marcus Aurelius, Charlemagne, Maria Theresa… a dozen or so small figures representing the city's heroes and heroines appear one by one at each hour and form a procession at noon.

Altes Rathaus (18)
Wipplinger Strasse 8, 1010

The Old City Hall (1699) has a façade in the style of Fischer von Erlach. Passing beneath one of the gateways flanked by figures of Justice and Right (Johann Martin Fischer), you reach an inner courtyard enclosing the fine Andromeda Fountain. In a niche surrounded by cherubs is the group sculpted in Italy by Georg Raphael Donner (1693–1741).

Maria am Gestade (19)
Salvatorgasse 12, 1010

The Church of Our Lady of the Riverbank, one of the jewels of Austrian Gothic, thrusts its pierced spire above the Tiefer Graben. Its soaring façade displays an elegant stone balustrade and two slender, sculpted pinnacles. The narrowness of the building and the fact that the nave is at an angle to the chancel is explained by the constraints of the site. Inside, there are splendid stained-glass windows, a 14th- or 15th-century Annunciation, Gothic retables and a Renaissance altar.

95

In the area
▶ **Where to stay:** ➡ 26 ➡ 30
▶ **Where to eat:** ➡ 46 ➡ 48
▶ **After dark:** ➡ 80 ➡ 82
▶ **Where to shop:** ➡ 146 ➡ 148–149

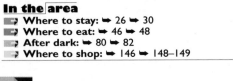

What to see

Freyung (20)
Freyung, 1010

Ⓜ U3, Herrengasse

The name (*frei* meaning 'free') refers to the right of asylum enjoyed by foreigners and thieves who took refuge in the Scottish Monastery. The Freyung is a large square, formerly used for popular festivals, but also for the execution of traitors, who were drowned head downward in a barrel. The so-called Scottish monastery and church (1155) were in fact founded by Irish monks summoned to Vienna by Heinrich II Jasomirgott, the first Duke of Austria. In the center of the square stands the Austria Fountain (1848): the four rivers of the old empire (the Danube, Elbe, Vistula and Po) surround the figure of Austria, for which Beethoven's granddaughter is said to have posed. The Kinsky Palace (1713–16) is one of the finest buildings by Johann Lukas von Hildebrandt.

Ferstel Palace (21)
Freyung 2, 1010

Ⓜ U3 Herrengasse ◯ Mon.–Sat. 6am–9pm; Sun. 10am–9pm

Built in 1856 for Heinrich von Ferstel combining Romanesque and Renaissance styles, the palace stands beside the Harrach Palace (1690) in the Herrengasse (Street of the Noblemen). This street is full of palaces – all the aristocrats of Lower Austria wanted theirs near the Hofburg – but the Ferstel is one of the few open to the public. Also worth a look is no. 23, the Porcia Palace (1546), one of the oldest palaces in Vienna and still retaining Renaissance features.

Am Hof (22)
Am Hof, 1010

Ⓜ U3 Herrengasse

The Märkleinisches Haus (18th century), designed by Von Hildebrandt, occupies the site of the medieval castle of the Babenbergs. In 1156 the German Emperor Barbarossa transformed the old Ostmark (East March) into a duchy. The first duke, Heinrich II Jasomirgott, a Babenberg, then transferred his court to Vienna, and the square was named appropriately Am Hof – the Court. Here, from the top of the church steps 700 years later (1806), the end of the Holy Roman Empire was officially proclaimed; Francis II of Habsburg would henceforth be known as Emperor Francis I of Austria, his hereditary possession. At the Collalto Palace (no. 13), Mozart made his first concert appearance aged six. In the center of the square, on the Virgin's Column (commemorating the Thirty Years War) angels doing battle with the four great scourges of humanity: the Plague (represented by a basilisk), Heresy (serpent), War (lion) and Famine (dragon). The Fire Department barracks and museum (no. 10) are in the former City Arsenal.

Not forgetting
■ **Uhrenmuseum (23)** Schulhofgasse 2, 1010 ☎ (1) 5332265 ◯ 9am–4.30pm *The museum houses one of the world's largest collections of clocks and horological instruments.* ■ **Kunstforum Bank of Austria (24)** Freyung 8, 1010 ☎ (1) 5332266 ◯ 10am–6pm; Wed. till 9pm *Retrospectives of 20th-century painters.*

Strength and Perseverance on top of the old Arsenal, now a fire station and firefighting museum.

In the area
➡ **Where to stay:** ➡ 18 ➡ 26 ➡ 36
➡ **Where to eat:** ➡ 46 ➡ 48 ➡ 50
➡ **After dark:** ➡ 68 ➡ 74 ➡ 76 ➡ 82
➡ **Where to shop:** ➡ 146

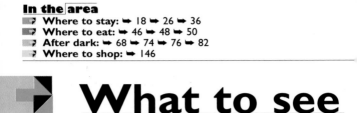

What to see

Burgtheater (25)
Dr-Karl-Lueger-Ring 2, 1010 ☎ (1) 514 44-2956

🚋 *1, 2, D, Burgtheater/Rathaus* 🕐 *Times subject to variation, announced 1 week ahead* ● *60 schillings*

In 1776, Joseph II began to reorganize the 'Court and National Theater' founded in 1741 by Maria Theresa on the Michaelerplatz. On the emperor's birthday in 1797, Haydn conducted a performance of his 'Emperor's Hymn', which was to become the Austrian National Anthem. The present building (1880) is in a mixture of Renaissance Revival, Baroque and Second Empire styles. Inside are frescos by Gustav Klimt and his brother Ernst.

Neues Rathaus (26)
Rathausplatz, 1010 ☎ (1) 52550

🚋 *1, 2, D, Burgtheater/Rathaus* 🕐 *Mon.,Wed., Fri. 1pm.* ● *admission free* 🚻

The public buildings of the Ring are steeped in the past, borrowing from the styles of every period – classical, Gothic, Renaissance, Baroque – as befits their particular purposes. The Ringstrasse, a peripheral boulevard constructed in place of the old city walls in the second half of the 19th century, appears as a triumph of Historicism and Eclecticism, and is virtually an ABC of Austria's architectural history. There are echoes of the Low Countries, with the New City Hall (neo-Gothic) inspired by that of Brussels and crowned by a 295-ft high bell tower. The council chambers, reception rooms and the grand saloon – where public balls are held – are open to visitors. There is a wonderful view from the tower.

The Church of the Minor Friars (27)
Minoritenplatz 2a, 1010

The Church of the Minor Friars, the first order founded by Saint Francis of Assisi (1182–1226), was originally a chapel, built shortly after the death of Saint Francis. It was later destroyed by fire and rebuilt in the 14th century in the Gothic style. Noteworthy features are the large portals sculpted with scenes of the Crucifixion (14th century) and, inside, the 15th-century bas-relief of the Virgin. In the sanctuary will be found the tomb of the Italian poet Metastasio (1698–1782), many of whose melodramas served as libretti for operatic composers. There is also a mosaic copy of Leonardo da Vinci's *Last Supper*, commissioned by Napoleon I, who intended to transfer the original from Milan to the Louvre, placing this copy in its stead.

Universität (28)
Dr-Karl-Renner-Ring 1, 1010

The University was created in 1365 by Rudolph II. Eventually it was moved out of the old city into this Renaissance Revival building which dates from 1873 to 1884. Busts of its most famous teachers, including Sigmund Freud, will be found in the central courtyard.

Not forgetting
■ **Votivkirche (29)** Rooseveltplatz, 1090 *The Votive Church, built in thanksgiving for Franz-Joseph's escape from assassination in 1853, is a neo-Gothic building with two soaring spires.*

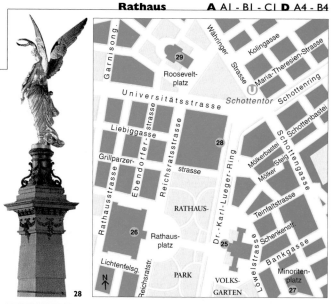

28

26

29

In the area
- **Where to stay:** ➜ 18 ➜ 26
- **Where to eat:** ➜ 40 ➜ 42 ➜ 46
- **After dark:** ➜ 74 ➜ 76 ➜ 80
- **Where to shop:** ➜ 130 ➜ 134 ➜ 138–139 ➜ 144 ➜ 148–149

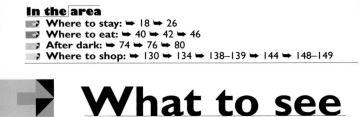

What to see

The Imperial Apartments (30)
Hofburg, Kaisertor, 1010 ☎ (1) 533 7570

🕐 Mon.–Sat. 8.30am–noon, 12.30–4pm; Sun. and public holidays 8.30am–12.30pm ● adults 80 schillings, concessions 40/60 schillings ♿

The Hofburg or Imperial Palace is virtually a city within a city, but only part is open to the public. Three major periods can be discerned in its construction… From the 13th to the 17th centuries, as long as Turkey posed a threat, the palace was more or less a fortress. In the 1700s it was enlarged and its appearance altered, thanks to a number of famous Baroque architects. Finally, in the 19th century, work on the Neue Burg (New Palace) was commenced in the direction of the Ring, reaching completion in 1914. The Leopold Wing, where Maria Theresa lived, is now the official residence of the President of the Austrian Republic. Three areas may be visited: (1) the apartments of Franz-Joseph, in the 18th-century Chancellery Wing designed by Fischer von Erlach; (2) the suite occupied by Empress Elisabeth, adjoining the Emperor's quarters in the oldest part of the complex, the Amalienburg; (3) the rooms used by Czar Alexander I during the Congress of Vienna, also in the Amalienburg.

Schatzkammer (31)
Schweizerhof, 1010 ☎ (1) 533 7931

Ⓜ U3, Herrengasse 🚋 D, J, 1, 2, Burgring Hofburg. 🕐 10am–6pm; closed Tue ● adults 100 schillings, concessions 70 schillings ♿

The Imperial Treasury contains many pieces of extraordinary interest for their beauty, age and semi-mythical associations. Among the relics of the Holy Roman Empire, look for the Holy Lance, borne in 935 by Otto I, when he led the Christian forces against the Magyars. Here too are numerous jewels and insignia, including the Imperial Crown, probably made at Reichenau for the coronation of Otto I in 962. Also on display is the treasure of the Habsburgs, as well as that of the Norman rulers of Sicily, the dukes of Burgundy and the Order of the Golden Fleece. It was through the system of dynastic alliances that these riches passed into the possession of the Austrian royal family.

Burgkapelle (32)
Hofburg Schweizerhof ☎ (1) 533 9927

Ⓜ U1, U2, U4 Karlsplatz 🚋 streetcar 1,2,D,J 🕐 Mon.–Thu. 11am–3pm, Fri. 11am–1pm **Sung Mass:** 🕐 Sun. and Holy Days, 9.15am ● 60/340 schillings, tickets on sale preceding Fri. 11am–1pm, 3–5pm

Every Sunday and Holy Day, Mass is sung by the Vienna Boys' Choir, which formed part of the Hofmusikkapelle (Court Orchestra) created in the 16th century by Maximilian I. When Austria became a republic, the state took over this world-famous institution, and 150 boys receive a first-class musical education at the Augarten Palace.

Neue Burg (33)
Heldenplatz, 1010 ☎ (1) 52524

🕐 10am–6pm; closed Tue ● 60 schillings, concessions 40 schillings ♿

The most recent part of the Hofburg contains several museums. The Ephesus section displays artefacts excavated at Ephesus and Samothrace.

Ballhaus-
platz

Schaufierg.

HOFBURG
30

Michaeler-
platz

Burgring

Helden-
platz

32

31

33

NEUE BURG

Josefs-
platz

30

30

30

Through the Schweizerhof (Swiss Courtyard) is the Schatzkammer which houses the fabulous treasures – both secular and sacred – of the Habsburgs.

30

30

Of the 2,600 rooms in the Imperial Palace, only a few are open to the public.

33

32

In the area

➡ **Where to stay:** ➡ 18 ➡ 26
➡ **Where to eat:** ➡ 40 ➡ 42 ➡ 46
➡ **After dark:** ➡ 74 ➡ 76 ➡ 80
➡ **Where to shop:** ➡ 132 ➡ 142 ➡ 144 ➡ 148–149

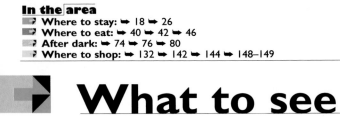

➡ What to see

Stallburg (34)
Reitschulgasse, 1010

Closed to the public.

Work is in progress to restore this fine Renaissance palace to its former glory. Ferdinand I commissioned it in 1558 for his son Maximilian; when the latter succeeded to the throne, he installed himself in the Old Palace, freeing the Stallburg for use as the royal stables. In 1562, Archduke Charles, his brother, set up an important stud at Lipizza, near Trieste, and imported the Spanish thoroughbreds which gave the renowned royal school its name: the Spanish Riding School. In the 1500s, deliberate interbreeding of these horses with others from Arabia and Dalmatia produced the famous Lipizzaner stallions, used both for military and ceremonial purposes.

Spanische Reitschule (35)
Michaelerplatz 1, 1010 ☎ (1) 535 0186

Dressage school: 🕒 *Feb. 15–June 25, Aug. 30–Oct. 8 and Nov. 16–Dec. 18, Tue.–Fri. 10am–noon (telephone in advance)* ● *adults 100 schillings, children 30 schillings* ***Equestrian Ballets*** 🕒 *variable; book at least 3 months in advance* ● *seats: adults 250–900 schillings, children 250 schillings, standing only, 200 schillings* ♿ @ *office@srs.at http://www.spanische-reitschule.com*

The Winter Manège, built between 1729 and 1735 by Joseph Emanuel Fischer von Erlach, is a magnificent example of Austrian Baroque. It not only formed a wonderful setting for equestrian ballets and carousels, but was also the scene of the state banquet for the marriage of Marie-Louise and Napoleon in 1810, as well as of balls and concerts during the Congress of Vienna (1815). From September until June, the public are allowed to watch the performances of the Spanish Riding School (Wed. evenings, Sat. and Sun. mornings).

Augustinerkirche (36)
Augustinerstrasse 3, 1010

The Augustinian Church is part of a large complex which also includes the Albertina and the hothouses. It was here that Anton Bruckner is said to have composed and given the first public performance of his Mass in F Minor. The musical tradition is still maintained: High Mass (Sun. 11am) is accompanied by an orchestra and first-rate choirs, performing mainly Austrian sacred music. Look for the tomb of the Archduchess Marie-Christine, daughter of Maria Theresa, by the Italian neoclassical sculptor Canova; also the crypt, where the hearts of the imperial family are preserved in silver urns.

Nationalbibliothek (37)
Josephplatz 1, 1010 ☎ 534 10

Ⓜ *U1, U2, U4 Karlsplatz* 🚋 *streetcar 1, 2, D, J* 🕒 *Mon.–Sat. 10am–2pm; closed Sun. and public holidays* ● *50 schillings* ♿ @ *http://www.onb.ac.at, oea@onb.ac.at*

The Court Library – later to become the National Library – was dispersed throughout the Hofburg before Charles VI commissioned a special building for the collection from Fischer von Erlach. Various sections are also housed in the Augustinian wing, the Albertina and the Neue Burg.

Between the Michaelerplatz and the Josefplatz are the fine monuments of Imperial Vienna, including the old Royal Church (Augustiner-kirche) where the Habsburg weddings were held.

In the area

➡ **Where to stay:** ➡ 18 ➡ 26 ➡ 34 ➡ 36
➡ **Where to eat:** ➡ 40 ➡ 46 ➡ 54
➡ **After dark:** ➡ 74 ➡ 76
➡ **Where to shop:** ➡ 130 ➡ 132 ➡ 138–139 ➡ 144 ➡ 146 ➡ 148–14

➡ What to see

Parliament (38)
Dr-Karl-Renner-Ring 3, 1010 ☎ (1) 401 10-0/401 10-30

🅼 U2, U3, Volkstheater 🚊 D, J, 1, 2, Stadiongasse/Parlament ● 40 schillings 🎫
🕐 Mon.–Fri. 11am and 3pm (except when Parliament in session); July 15–Sep.15
Mon.–Fri. 9am, 11am, 1pm, 2pm, 3pm; Sat. and Sun. by appointment ♿

The Parliament Building dates from 1784 to 1883. Its architect, Theophil
von Hansen, drew his inspiration from classical Greece, the cradle of
democracy, crowning the building with four-horse chariots driven by
winged figures of Victory. The statues on the steps are of ancient
historians. The fountain in front of the building is dwarfed by a giant
Pallas Athene, representing political wisdom. It was before the Parliament
Building in 1918 that the Austrian Republic was proclaimed.

Kunsthistorisches Museum (39)
Maria-Theresien-Platz, 1010 ☎ (1) 52524

🅼 U2, Babenbergerstrasse 🚊 D, J, 1, 2, Burgring 🕐 10am–6pm, Thu. 10am–9pm;
closed Mon. ● adults 100 schillings, concessions 70 schillings 🎫 10.30am (in
German), 11.15am (English) ● 30 schillings ♿ @ info@khm.at
http://www.khm.at

Vienna's Museum of Art History is one of the richest in Europe. Its
collection is divided into five sections: Egyptian and Oriental Antiquities;
Greek, Roman and Etruscan Antiquities; Sculpture and Decorative Arts
(Medieval, Renaissance, Baroque); Coins and Medals; and finally, the *pièce de
résistance*, the Art Department. Italian, Spanish, French and German schools
are well represented, but it is the Flemish and Dutch works which are the
jewels in the crown of the Kunsthistorisches. Vienna, in fact, is the place to
see Peter Bruegel (the Elder), since over a quarter of his output is housed
in this museum. It is also the best place to enjoy Rubens, Van Dyck and the
Flemish Primitives – not forgetting, of course, works such as Vermeer's *The
Artist in his Studio* and Rembrandt's *Larger Self-Portrait*. The Kunsthistorisches
owes its opulence to the policies of the Habsburgs – insatiable collectors
from the first 'Cabinet Room of Arts and Wonders' set up by Ferdinand I in
the 16th century to the acquisitions of his nephew Rudolph and the
Archduke Leopold-William.

Naturhistorisches Museum (40)
Burgring, 1010 ☎ (1) 52177

🅼 U2, Babenbergerstrasse 🚊 D, J, 1,2, Burgring 🕐 10am–6pm, Thu. till 9pm; closed
Mon. ● adults 100 schillings, concessions 70 schillings 🎫 10.30am (German),
11.15am (English) ● 30 schillings ♿ 🔬 @ oeff.arbeit@nhm-wien.ac.at

The Natural History Museum houses comprehensive collections of rock
and mineral specimens, as well as of prehistoric artefacts, including the
Wiliendorf Venus, a 25,000-year-old fertility symbol.

Not forgetting
Museumsquartier (41) Museumsplatz 1, 1010 *The former court stables,
built between 1719 and 1723, are set to accommodate a huge museum complex –
Europe's largest cultural center – from the year 2001.*

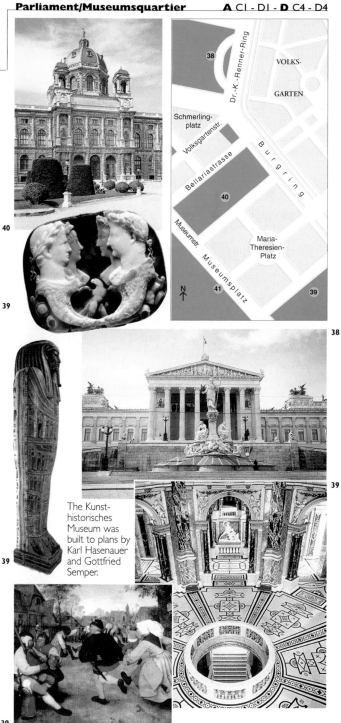

40

39

The Kunst-
historisches
Museum was
built to plans by
Karl Hasenauer
and Gottfried
Semper.

39

38

39

39

39

The Wiener Secession (1897–1907) was a movement formed at the Academy of Fine Arts by young painters, architects and decorative artists, mainly pupils of Otto Wagner. Its intention was to break with the Historicist art forms as symbolized by the Ringstrasse buildings; its members 'seceded' from the traditional Artists' House Association.

What to see

Secession Building (42)
Friedrichstrasse 12, 1010 ☎ (1) 587 5307

Ⓜ U2, U4 Karlsplatz 🕐 Tue.–Sat. 10am–6pm; Sun. 10am–4pm ● 60 schillings

The best of Joseph Maria Olbrich's talent was poured into this pavilion designed for exhibitions of Viennese avant-garde art. It was the flagship of the Secessionist movement. Its façade carried a provocative message ('To every age its art, to art its liberty'), and its architecture combined geometrical rigor with sumptuous orientalism. Damaged during World War Two and subsequently abandoned, it was later restored to house exhibitions of contemporary art. It has also regained its Beethoven frieze, which once more occupies all four walls of a large room.

Leopoldskirche am Steinhof (43)
Baumgartner Höhe, 1140 ☎ (1) 91060-20031

🚌 Bus 48A da Dr Karl Renner Ring/U3 Volkstheater 🕐 daily 3pm, 4pm (English); Sat., Sun. by appointment 🎫 guided tours only

This is a neo-Byzantine reinterpretation of the Karlskirche (Church of St Leopold), perched on a hill in the grounds of the Am Steinhof Psychiatric Hospital. Cubist interpretation of space, predilection for geometrical pattern and straight lines, flat decorative effects, opulent facings … the Secessionists' blend of severity and ornamentalism in some ways prefigures Art Deco.

Museum für angewandte Kunst (44)
Stubenring 5, 1010 ☎ (1) 71136-0

Ⓜ U3, Stubentor, U4, Landstrasse 🚃 streetcar 1, 2, Stubentor 🕐 10am–6pm (Thu. 10am–9pm), closed Mon. ● 30 schillings 🍴 🍷 ♿ ⊞ @ office@mak.at, http://www.MAK.at

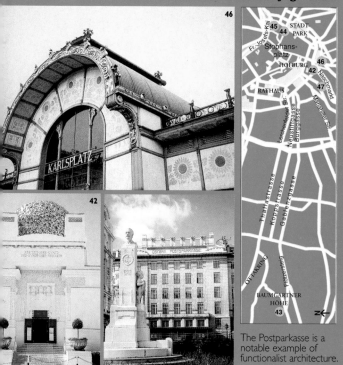

The Postparkasse is a notable example of functionalist architecture.

The Museum of Applied Arts, established in 1864 and entirely renovated in 1993, houses collections of old furniture, ceramics, carpets and textiles as well as gold- and silverware (16th–19th centuries). Also to be seen are numerous examples of Jugendstil pieces, mainly by the Wiener Werkstätten, the Viennese studio founded in 1897 by Joseph Hoffman and Koloman Moser.

Zentrale Postsparkasse (45)
Georg-Coch-Platz 2, 1010

M *U 3, Stubentor* **⊞** *1, 2 Stubenring*

The earliest building of its type on the Ring, the Postparkasse (1904–6) illustrates a functionalist approach which was to become one of the fundamental tenets of the Modern Movement.

Stadtbahn Pavillions/Stations de métro (46)
Karlsplatz, 1010

M *U2, U4 Karlsplatz/Oper* **◐** *9.15am–12.15pm and 1–4.30pm; closed Mon.*

Otto Wagner, commissioned by the municipal authorities (1898–9) to provide new facilities for the city's public transport system, designed a series of some thirty subway stations. The example in the Karlsplatz is particularly worth seeing – a utilitarian building, yet elegant and refined. Wagner also made use of modern techniques: the decorative floral panels were mass-produced and mounted on prefabricated metal structures.

Not forgetting

■ Wienzeile Houses (47) *Constructed around 1898–9 by Otto Wagner, the dwelling houses of the Linke Wienzeile (nos. 16, 38 and 40) are excellent examples of Jugendstil.*

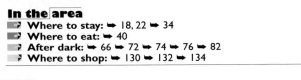

What to see

Gemäldegalerie der Akademie der bildenden Künste (48)
Schillerplatz 3, 1010 ☎ (1) 58816

Ⓜ U1, U2, U4, Karlsplatz 🚋 streetcar 1, 2, D, J, Oper 🕓 Tue.–Sun. 10am–4pm
● adults 50 schillings, concessions 20 schillings

The gallery is to be found in a wing of the Academy of Fine Arts, and contains several very interesting works, including the triptych of the *Last Judgment* by Hieronymus Bosch. There is a good, representative selection of Flemish painters, also of Italian artists of the 18th century.

Wiener Staatsoper (49)
Opernring 2, 1010 ☎ (1) 514 442955/56

Ⓜ U2, U4 🚋 D, J, 1, 2, Karlsplatz/Oper 🎫 see programs in theater arcade (Kärntner Strasse) ● 60 schillings ♿

Under Leopold I (1659–1705), Vienna had become one of the foremost European centers of music and theater. In 1794, the first venue devoted to opera and ballet was established at no. 4, Philharmonikerstrasse, behind the present-day Opera. 1893 saw the inauguration of the new Opera House with a performance of Mozart's *Don Giovanni*. Under the leadership of Mahler and later Richard Strauss, the company enjoyed decades of success. Closed in the summer of 1944, the Opera was destroyed in the following year by the Russian bombardments. Rebuilt to the original plan by Erich Boltenstern, it ceremonially reopened its doors in 1955, some months after the signing of the treaty which restored full sovereignty to Austria. For the occasion, Karl Böhm conducted a performance of Beethoven's only opera, *Fidelio*.

Albertina Graphische Sammlung (50)
Augustinerstrasse, 1010 ☎ (1) 53483-0

@ info@albertina.ac.at, http://www.albertina.at/albertina

The Albertina houses the collection of engravings, drawings and watercolors formerly belonging to Duke Albert of Saxe-Teschen (hence the name), husband of the Archduchess Marie-Christine and son-in-law of Maria Theresa and the print collection of Prince Eugene. With more than a million engravings, 44,000 drawings and watercolors, it is the world's most important collection of graphic art. But the interest of the exhibits also lies in their quality; the Rembrandt and Rubens collection is virtually unique, that of Dürer's work undoubtedly so. The Austrian school is, of course, extremely well represented. The scale of the collection means that works are normally displayed on a rotating basis or in temporary exhibitions. The museum is closed for restoration at the time of going to press, but small-scale exhibitions can be viewed at the Akademiehof, Markartgasse 3/1010 (near the Secession Building).

Not forgetting

Kapuzinergruft (51) Neuer Markt, 1010 ☎ (1) 535 0431 Ⓜ U1, U3, Stephansplatz, U2, U4 Karlsplatz 🚋 D, J, 1, 2 Karlsplatz 🕓 9.30am–4pm *The Kaisergruft (Imperial Vaults) and the Kapuzinergruft (Capuchin Crypt), to the left of the Capuchin Church, contain the tombs and memorials of 145 members of the imperial family, traditionally buried here since 1633.*

Dürer's famous *Hare* is one of the artist's 145 drawings kept at the Albertina.

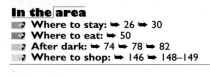

What to see

Freud Haus (52)
Berggasse 19, 1090 ☎ (1) 319 1596

🚋 *streetcar D Schlickgasse, streetcar 37, 38, 40, 41, 42 Schwarzspanierstrasse* 🕐 *July–Sep. 9am–6pm; Oct.–June 9am–4pm* ● *60 schillings*

Two stories of this plush apartment building on the Berggasse provided Sigmund Freud with both home and consulting rooms for over half a century (1856–1938). It was here too that he wrote his revolutionary papers on psychiatry. The building is now a museum, and contains some of Freud's original furniture. The couch, however, is merely symbolic: the real one was removed by the founder of psychoanalysis when he fled to London from the Nazis in 1938.

Museum moderner Kunst (53)
Palazzo Liechtenstein, Fürstengasse 1, 1090 ☎ (1) 317 6900

🚋 *streetcar D Bauernfeldplatz* 🕐 *10am–6pm; closed Mon.* ● *45 schillings* ♿ @ *museum@MMKSLW.or.at, http://www.MMKSLW.or.at/MMKSLW*

The Museum of Modern Art occupies the former Summer Palace of the Princes of Liechtenstein (17th century). The decoration of the interior owes much to the work of famous artists of various schools, as can be seen from the Rottmayr frescos in the vestibule and the Giovanni Pozzo ceiling in the main reception room. Most modern art movements are represented, from Surrealism and Expressionism to Abstract Art and the neo-Realists – Max Ernst, Munch, Kandinsky, Hartung and Andy Warhol all figure here – but the visitor will probably be most fascinated by the Austrians: Kokoschka, Schiele, Klimt, Hundertwasser… The Museum also organizes temporary exhibitions of the latest trends in contemporary art.

Schubert Haus (54)
Nussdorfer Strasse 54, 1090 ☎ 317 3601

🚋 *streetcar 37, 38 Nussdorfer Strasse* 🕐 *9am–12.15pm, 1–4.30pm: closed Mon.* ● *25 schillings*

No music-lover can pass through the Austrian capital without paying tribute to that most Viennese of composers, Franz Schubert. When he was born on January 31, 1797, the family occupied three rooms overlooking a courtyard at the sign of the Red Crawfish. This schoolmaster's son enjoyed a better musical education than has hitherto been claimed, as he was a choirboy at the Imperial Chapel. As an adult, he shared lodgings with one friend after another and remained addicted to the life of café and tavern. From 1822, his health began to deteriorate. He died at the age of 31 on November 10, 1828 in a wretched little room at no. 6 Kettengasse (open to the public). He is laid to rest in the Zentralfriedhof (Central Cemetery) in company with Beethoven, Brahms and Johann Strauss I and II.

Josephinum (55)
Währingerstrasse 25, 1 ☎ (1) 427 763401

Ⓜ *U2 Schottentor* 🚋 *streetcar 37, 38, 40, 41, 42 Schwarzspanierstrasse* 🕐 *Mon.–Fri. 9am–3pm (except public holidays)* ● *20 schillings*

The former Military Academy of Medicine and Surgery was founded by Joseph II on the model of the Hôtel Dieu in Paris.

The houses where Franz Schubert and Sigmund Freud lived have been turned into museums.

In the area
➡ **Where to stay:** ➡ 20 ➡ 32
➡ **Where to eat:** ➡ 58 ➡ 60
➡ **After dark:** ➡ 66 ➡ 74 ➡ 76
➡ **Where to shop:** ➡ 130 ➡ 148–149

➡ What to see

Karlskirche (56)
Karlsplatz, 1040

Ⓜ *U2, U4 Karlsplatz*

The Church of St Charles was commissioned from Fischer von Erlach by Charles VI on the ending of the plague epidemic of 1713. But this is more than a votive church: it is also a glorious symbol of the temporal power of the Holy Roman emperors and the Catholic faith which they defended. It is dedicated to Saint Charles Borromeo, Bishop of Milan, for his devotion to duty during the plague of 1576 and for his role in the Council of Trent. Seen from the exterior, the church resembles a great Italian Renaissance basilica, onto which has been grafted a portico worthy of the Roman forum. More innovative is the framing of the dome between two triumphal columns inspired by those of Trajan and Marcus Aurelius. Inside, note the fresco in the oval cupola – on the left you will see an angel burning Luther's celebrated bible.

Historisches Museum der Stadt Wien (57)
Karlsplatz, 1040 ☎ (1) 505 8747-84021

Ⓜ *U2, U4 Karlsplatz* 🕐 *Tue.–Sun. 9am–6pm* ● *50 schillings* ♿

The three-story City Historical Museum retraces Vienna's past from the first human settlements up to the present. With the aid of photographs, pictures, plans, models, realistic recreations, artefacts from digs and objets d'art, the visitor can follow the city's development and the changing patterns of Viennese life.

Österreichische Galerie Belvedere (58)
Prinz-Eugen-Strasse 27, 1030 ☎ (1) 79557

🚋 *streetcar D Schloss Belvedere, 71 Salesianergasse* 🕐 *10am–5pm; closed Mon. Guided tours:* ☎/➡ *(1) 79557-134* @ *public@belvedere.at* ● *60 schillings* 🎴 ♿

When Eugène de Savoie-Carignan (1663–1736) was refused command of a regiment by Louis XIV, he placed himself at the service of Austria. For his Summer Palace, he turned to Lukas von Hildebrandt. In 1716, the Unteres (Lower) Belvedere reached completion. A few years later, Hildebrandt added a second building, on higher ground, destined for receptions and official functions: the Oberes (Upper) Belvedere, more splendid still, more baroque and oriental, and separated from the first construction by a French-style garden. The Lower Belvedere houses the fascinating Museum of Austrian Baroque Art, while the Museum of Medieval Austrian Art is located in the Orangery. The Gallery of 19th- and 20th-Century Austrian Art, which has occupied the Upper Belvedere since 1953, is particularly noteworthy for a magnificent collection of Klimts and important works by Egon Schiele, Kokoschka and Gerstl.

Museum moderner Kunst (59)
20er Haus Arsenalgasse 1, 1030 ☎ (1) 799 6900

🚋 *streetcar D, O, autobus 13A, 18 Südbanhof.* 🕐 *Tue.–Sun. 10am–6pm* ● *45 schillings* ♿ @ *museum@MMKSLW.or.at, http://www.MMKSLW.or.at/MMKSLW*

The collections of 20th-century art housed here, together with those from the Liechtenstein Palace, will soon be placed on display at the Museumsquartier, which is currently undergoing alterations ➡ 104.

In 1857, Franz-Joseph signed the order for the demolition of the outer fortifications. The ramparts – a favorite promenading place for 19th-century Viennese – gave way to the Ringstrasse, a broad peripheral boulevard bordered with parks and gardens which, with the Wienerwald (Vienna Woods), help to make Vienna one of the 'greenest' cities in Europe.

What to see

Stadtpark (60)
Parkring, 1010

🕐 *always open*

The Municipal Park (1862) is laid out in English style around the River Wien; swans, flamingos and peacocks have free run of the place. There is a network of walks among groves of every kind; now and then, turning a corner, you will come upon statues of Franz Schubert, Hans Makart, Robert Stolz, Anton Bruckner and other great figures from the cultural world of 19th-century Vienna. Best known is that of Johann Strauss the Younger (1921): Edmund Heller designed it with a band of naiads swirling about the gilt-bronze figure of the composer, who is playing his violin. Just opposite, concerts of waltz music are given in the summer months on the terrace of the Kursalon (Pump-Room).

Burggarten (61)
Opernring, 1010

🕐 *Apr. 1–Sep. 30: 6am–10pm; Oct. 1–Mar. 31: 6am–8pm*

The Imperial Gardens, once the promenade of the Imperial Court, were opened to the public in 1919. Visitors are welcomed by a statue of Mozart. At the very end of the garden are the hothouses – part of a large complex including the Albertina and the Augustinerkirche. The Palmenhaus has recently been refurbished; on entering your heart will leap like a child's at the first glimpse of the tropical butterflies

The famous gilt-bronze statue of Johann Strauss the Younger in the Stadtpark.

62

63

60

(⏱ 10am–4pm, 70 schillings, concessions 40 schillings). A café-restaurant has also been opened in an annex.

Volksgarten (62)
Dr-Karl-Renner-Ring, 1010

⏱ Apr.1–Sep. 30: 6am–10pm; Oct. 1–Mar. 31: 6am–8pm

The Volksgarten was opened to the public as early as 1809. In the center of this park renowned for its roses stands the Temple of Theseus (Nobile, 1820) – a scale replica of the Theseion in Athens – used for temporary exhibitions. The Meierei café (Apr.–Sep.: 8am–9pm) provides a welcome refuge from a shower. In front of the café is the statue of the dramatist Grillparzer, and, at the end of the garden, one of the Empress Sissi, assassinated in Switzerland in 1898.

Rathauspark (63)
Rathausplatz, 1010

⏱ always open

A wide avenue flanked by statues of Vienna's great and good leads through this park, which faces the City Hall. The gardens are a favorite meeting-place for Viennese. In the winter, they flock to the skating rink and the Christmas market.

60

61

In the area
➡ **Where to stay:** ➡ 30 ➡ 32
➡ **Where to eat:** ➡ 60
➡ **After dark:** ➡ 74
➡ **Where to shop:** ➡ 148

➡ What to see

Riesenrad/The giant Ferris wheel (1)
Praterstern, 1020 ☎ (1) 729 5430

🕐 *Nov. 3–Jan. 12, Feb. 11–28: 10am–6pm; Mar. 1–Apr. 30: 10am–10pm; May 1–Sep. 30: 9am–midnight; Oct. 1–Nov. 3: 10am–10pm* ● *adults 55 schillings, children (3–14 yrs) 20 schillings* 🔲 🍴 🏢 🔲 *Café Frederik* ♿

This imposing steel structure weighing 475 tonnes and nearly 215 ft high was designed by an Englishman, W. Basset, and built in 1897 for the fiftieth anniversary of Franz-Joseph's coronation. With the Stephansdom, the Prater's Ferris wheel is the symbol of Vienna. Since it revolves at only 1½ ft per second, you have plenty of time to admire the panoramic view of the city and its surroundings.

Wurstelprater (2)

🕐 *see Riesenrad* 🏨 *Schweizerhaus Strasse des 1. Mai, 116 ☎ (1) 728 0152* 🕐 *Mar. 15–Oct. 31: daily 10am–11pm*

Even before the giant wheel was built, there was no shortage of attractions on the Prater; it was used for theatrical performances, and, from 1774, for firework displays. The name Wurstelprater doesn't mean that the place is devoted to consuming those famous sausages! In fact, it recalls Hans Wurst, a traditional, tragi-comic clown. Its great days may be over, but the funfair remains a popular place to unwind and meet friends. The Schweizerhaus is one of the city's most frequented brasseries – make sure you try the delicious grilled ham.

Grüner Prater (3)

Ⓜ *U1 Praterstern* 🚌 *bus 77A, 80A, 80B, 82A*

Starting from the Praterstern, it is an easy walk along the three miles of the Prater Hauptallee, the Park's main avenue lined with ancient chestnut trees. Traffic is banned; walkers, joggers and roller-bladers share space quite happily. Beyond the trees on each side are grassy meadows where you can picnic, play ball or just laze around.

Hundertwasserhaus (4)
Kegelgasse 36-38, 1080

Galleria Kunsthaus Wien Untere Weissgerberstrasse, 13 🕐 *adults 90 schillings; children, students under 27 and senior citizens 60 schillings* 🔲 🏢 🔲 ♿

The Viennese painter Friedensreich Hundertwasser intended this highly unconventional experiment in popular architecture as a protest against the monotony of urban constructions. His eccentric style is characterized by his rainbow-like use of color and by a feverish imagination which refuses to conform to established principles. His work may be viewed in the Kunsthaus Wien, close to the Hundertwasserhaus.

Not forgetting

■ **Lusthaus** *Prater Hauptallee/Freudenau, 254* ☎ *02 189565* 🕐 *Sat., Sun. and public holidays noon–6pm; May–Sep.: Mon., Tue., Thu., Fri. noon–11pm; Oct. and Apr.: daily noon–6pm; closed Wed. Originally an octagonal hunting lodge, now a first-class restaurant with a wonderful terrace.*

The scene of glittering spectacles and society functions during the Congress of Vienna, the Prater remains a favorite spot for the Viennese, with its vast green spaces, its attractions and sporting facilities.

In the area
➡ **Where to stay:** ➡ 34
➡ **Where to eat:** ➡ 54 ➡ 56
➡ **After dark:** ➡ 72 ➡ 74
➡ **Where to shop:** ➡ 148

➡ What to see

Schloss Schönbrunn (5)
1130 ☎ (1) 81113-0

🕐 *Ticket office: Apr.–Oct.: 8.30am–5pm; Nov.–Mar.: 8.30am–4.30pm*
● ***Imperial Tour*** *adults 90 schillings, children (6–15) 40 schillings, students (under 25) 80 schillings* ● ***Grand Tour*** *120 schillings, children (6–15) 50 schillings, students (under 25) 105 schillings* 📷 📹 ***Grand tour only*** *25 schillings* 🍴 *Café Residenz* 📷 ♿ 🚌 ⛷ *from the Gloriette*

After his victory over the Turks in 1683, Leopold I commissioned architect Fischer von Erlach to draw up plans for a summer residence to eclipse every other royal home. Work started in 1696, but was not to finish until 1749 under the direction of Nikolaus von Pacassi. After passing through the impressive Haupttor (main gate), you find yourself in the Ehrenhof (central courtyard), which immediately gives an idea of the sheer scale of the complex. Of the palace's 1,441 rooms, only 42 are open to visitors: the Imperial Tour takes in 22 rooms in the West Wing – state and reception rooms which are a triumph of 18th-century Rococo. The Grand Tour gives access to the 42 rooms, including some in the East Wing, where the Empress Maria Theresa lived.

Wagenburg (6)

🕐 *Apr.–Oct.: 9am–6pm; Nov.–Mar.: Tue.–Sun. 10am–4pm* ● *adults 30 schillings, children under 10 free, students (under 25) and senior citizens 15 schillings* 📷
🚌 🍴 *Kutschergwölb* ♿

The former winter riding-school now houses a fine collection of carriages, sleds and sedan chairs used at the Imperial Court from 1690 to 1918.

Park and Gloriette (7)

🕐 *6am–sunset*

The south front of the castle looks onto a formal garden whose strict geometric design gradually softens as you climb the slope, finally blending into more 'natural' vegetation. The eye comes to rest on the Gloriette, a neoclassical pavilion on the top of the slope, built to celebrate the victory over the Prussians at Kolin in 1757. As you climb toward the belvedere, you will pass the handsome Neptune Fountain; to the left of this, somewhat hidden by trees and bushes, is the Schöner Brunnen, or 'Beautiful Spring', after which the castle is named.

Tiergarten/Zoo (8)
☎ 877 92 94

🕐 *Nov.–Jan.: 9am–4.30pm; Feb. and Oct.: 9am–5pm; Mar.: 9am–5.30pm; Apr.: 9am–6pm; May–Sep.: 9am–6.30pm* ● *adults 45 schillings, children (3–6) 20 schillings, students (under 27) 30 schillings* 📷 📹 *Sun. 10am* 🚌 🍴 *Tirolergarten* ♿

This is Europe's oldest zoo, dating from 1752. Children will love it; some of the animals can be fed and stroked.

Not forgetting

■ **Café Meierei** Kronprinzengarten 🕐 *Apr.–Oct.: 10am–9pm A café in the park, with a pleasant garden (cool and shady).* ■ **Café Gloriette** Gloriette 🕐 *9am–6pm. Enjoy the cakes and petits fours while admiring the views of Schönbrunn and Vienna.*

Although trained in Italy, Fischer von Erlach modeled his plans on Versailles. The project which he presented to Leopold in 1690 actually surpassed the French palace in sheer size.

By boat or bus
Information on all excursions from Vienna
can be obtained from the Office of
Tourism, Kärntner Strasse 38
☎ (1) 513 8892 ⏱ 9am–7pm.

Further afield

A stone's throw from the city center...

Only 10 minutes from the city center, the Donauinsel (Danube Island) forms an immense leisure area. You meet crowds of cyclists and rollerbladers, but it is also popular for swimming and picnics on the long beach which borders the New Danube.  M *U1 Donauinsel*

7 Days out

THE INSIDER'S FAVORITES

A city in the countryside

Hikers or naturists, amateur sportsmen or experienced swimmers, there is something for everyone on the Old Danube (*Alte Donau*) and the Island of Gänselhäufel.
M *U1 Kaisermühlen*
Farther afield, the Lobau is a nature reserve which you can tour on foot or by bike (9-mile circuit ⏱ 1h30) featuring woodland, lakes and Napoleonic memorials (Battle of Essling).
M *U1 Kagran*, thence 🚌 *bus 26A to Gross-Enzersdorf*

Walks in the Vienna Woods

Astonishingly unspoiled, the Wienerwald, with its forests, spa towns and vineyards, is best explored on foot. A 'Beethoven trail' (*Beethoven-Spaziergang*, ⏱ 1 day) has been established from Baden to Mödling via Gumpoldskirchen, taking in places familiar to the composer. Maps and selected route-plans are available from the Office of Tourism, Hauptplatz 2, Baden.
☎ *(2) 252 86800*
🚆 *from Wien Mitte*
🚄 *from the Südbahnhof*

All the places mentioned in this section are easily accessible, even without a car, thanks to the excellence of the public transport system. Those who have time – and a good pair of legs – could do worse than try the bicycle track which runs all the way along the Austrian Danube: take the train to Melk from the Westbahnhof, or from the Franz-Josefs-

Further afield

Dürnstein
Krems

Gumpolds-kirchen (1)

🚌 Freeway A2 (Südautobahn) Baden exit.
🕐 30 mins
🚆 Lines S1 or S2 (Schnellbahn) (Wiener Neustadt direction) from the Wien Mitte/Landstrasse station (U3/U4) or from Meidling (U6). 🕐 35 mins
● 57 schillings)

Baden (2)

🚌 Freeway A2 (Südautobahn) Baden exit.
🕐 Allow 40 mins
🚆 Trains leave the Südbahnhof for Baden every 15 mins. 🕐 25 mins ● 57 schillings
🚋 Badner Bahn Departures from the Staatsoper.
🕐 Allow 1 hr
● 57 schillings

Heiligen-kreuz (3), Mayerling (4)

🚌 Freeway A2 (Südautobahn). Leave at Baden and proceed by the Helenental.
🕐 Allow 1hr
🚌 There is a daily bus service from Vienna to Heiligenkreuz.
🕐 Allow 90 mins
● 76 schillings

From Baden take the bus to Mayerling.
🕐 Allow 45 mins
● 38 schillings

Melk (5)

🚌 Freeway A1, Melk exit.
🕐 Allow 1 hr
🚆 From the

1

2

3

Bahnhof to Krems or Dürnstein. Bicycles can be rented and returned at any station.

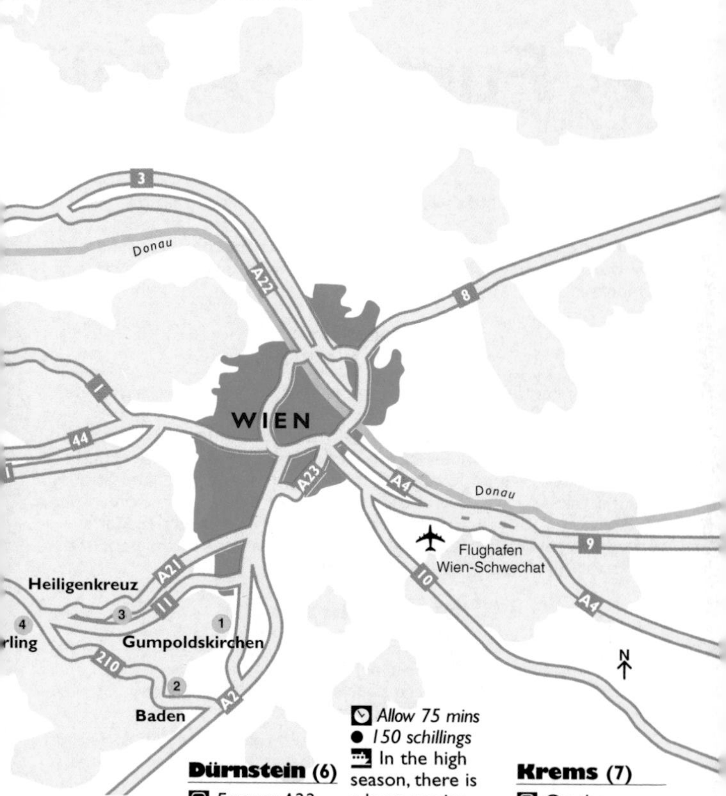

WIEN

Donau

Heiligenkreuz

Gumpoldskirchen

rling

Baden

Flughafen
Wien-Schwechat

Westbahnhof, regular service via St Pölten and Linz: change at St Pölten.
🕐 Allow 70 mins
● 150 schillings
From Melk station, walk or take a taxi to the abbey. 🕐 10 mins
● 60-70 schillings

Dürnstein (6)
🚗 Freeway A22 (Donauuferauto-bahn) as far as Tulln, then B3
🕐 Allow 75 mins
🚆 Daily service from the Franz-Josefs-Bahnhof; change at Krems.

🕐 Allow 75 mins
● 150 schillings
🚢 In the high season, there is a boat service every Sunday to Dürnstein from the Wien Reichbrücke.
🕐 May 2–Oct. 3; depart 8.45am, arrive 2.30pm.
● 260 schillings

Krems (7)
🚗 On the Dürnstein road.
🕐 Allow 1 hr
🚆 Through trains from the Franz-Josefs-Bahnhof.
🕐 Allow 1 hr
● 152 schillings

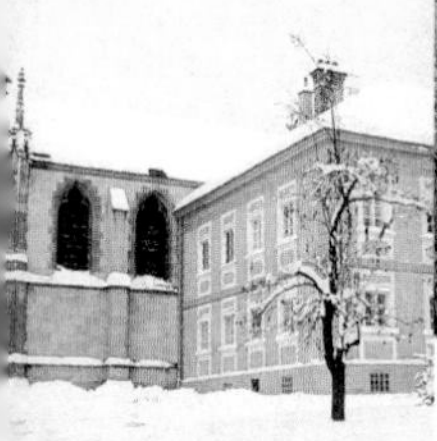

4

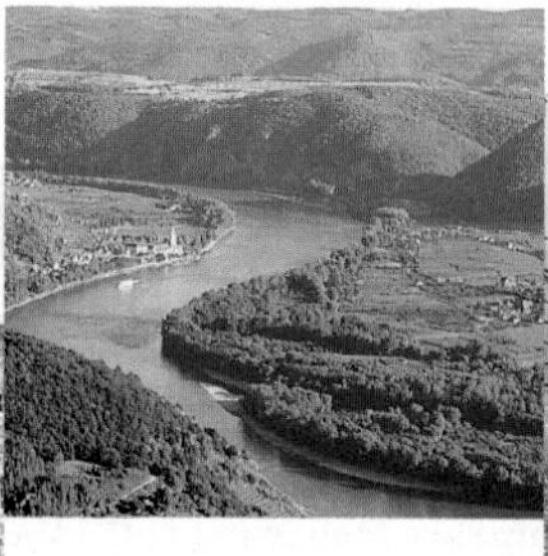

6

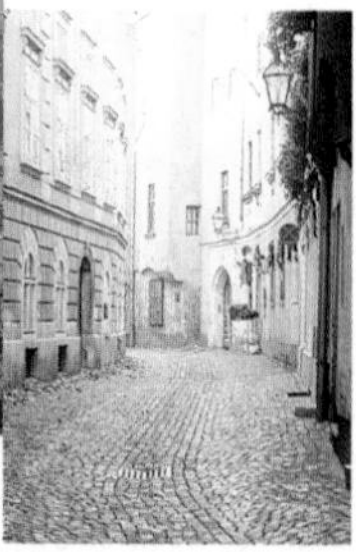

7

South of Vienna, the scowling suburbs slowly give way to a gentle landscape of hills clothed with vines and forests. You can have great fun trying out the local wines in the *Heurigen* – typical village inns. Nature lovers can follow a network of paths leading out into the vineyards and countryside of the Wienerwald.

Further Afield

Gumpoldskirchen (9)
☎ (02252) 62421

In this picturesque little village, centuries-old cellars attest the permanence of the area's wine-growing tradition. The Michaelskirche, dominating the village, is a starting-point for interesting walks; but you may choose to linger in one of the numerous *Heurigen* with a glass of *Gumpoldskirchner*, a well known local wine.

Baden (10)
☎ (02252) 44531/59

In the 19th century, this spa town served as a summer resort for the high society of Vienna. These were its golden years; most of its apartment buildings and palaces date from the first half of that century and are exquisite examples of the Biedermeier style. Among countless famous visitors were Mozart, Schubert, Beethoven and Johann Strauss. The thermal springs were already known and exploited in Roman times; nowadays the town boasts modern hydrotherapy centers (Baden's waters are particularly effective against rheumatism), a vast park with a casino and, in summer, an open-air theater.

Heiligenkreuz (11)
☎ (02258) 8703/33

🕒 *Mon.–Sat. 10am–5pm; Sun. and public holidays 11am–5pm*
● *adults 65 schillings, children and students 30 schillings* 🖾 🛢 *only*
10am, 11am, 2pm, 3pm, 4pm 🎫 🍴 *Stiftsgasthaus*

The Abbey of the Holy Cross, in a southern area of the Vienna Woods, is one of the most important of the Babenbergs' religious foundations. It has been in existence since 1133 when Margrave Leopold III established twelve Cistercian monks on the site. The new monastery was also intended to serve as his burial place. The architecture of the church – Romanesque in its triple-aisled basilican plan, but with Gothic apse and transepts – is a fine example of a transitional style.

Mayerling (12)
☎ (02258) 2275

🕒 *Mon.–Sat. 9am–12.30pm, 1.30–6pm; Sun. and public holidays 10am–12.30pm, 1.30–6pm (Oct.–Mar. till 5pm); stairs to bell tower at right of entrance*
● *adults 20 schillings, children (over 6) 10 schillings;* 🛢 *only* 🎫

In January 1889, in what was then a hunting lodge, Archduke Rudolph, the only son of Emperor Franz-Joseph, committed suicide at the age of thirty along with his teenage mistress Maria Vetsera (17). Ever since, Mayerling has been symbolic of the decline of the Habsburgs, and the place still retains a powerful atmosphere.

Not forgetting

■ **Hotel Sauerhof-Restaurant Rauhenstein (13)**, Weilburgstrasse, 11-13, Baden ☎ (02252) 41251 🕒 6–11pm *Excellent food in Biedermeier-style surroundings.* ■ **Kronprinz Mayerling (14)**, Mayerling ☎ (02258) 2378 🕒 Wed.–Sun. noon–3pm, 6.30pm–midnight. *Refined menu and a remarkable choice of wines and liquors.*

10

11

12

9

9

10

Its landscapes, art treasures and history make the picturesque Wachau region a wonderful center for days out. The region boasts the oldest surviving traces of human existence and the outstanding abbey of Melk. The grapes which will be used to produce Austria's finest white wines ripen in local vineyards.

Further afield

Melk Abbey (15)
☎ (02752) 52312/232

🕙 *From Palm Sunday to All Saints Day: 1 Apr. and Oct.: 9am–5pm (last admissions 4pm); May–Sep.: 9am–6pm (last admissions 5pm)* ● *adults 65 schillings, senior citizens 60 schillings, students (under 27) 30 schillings; families with children under 15 yrs 130 schillings* 🎫 *10am–3pm; May–Sep.10am—4pm, every hour, in German or according to demand; tickets 20 schillings* ♒ 🏢 🍴 *Stiftsrestaurant Melk* ♿

Today the abbey which symbolizes the flowering of Austrian Baroque stands majestically on a hill overlooking the Danube. In the Middle Ages, the site was occupied by the earliest residence of the dukes of Babenberg. In 1089, the family sold their chateau to the Benedictines, who turned it into a fortified abbey. In the early years of the 18th century, Abbot Dietmayr entrusted the architect Jakob Prandtauer with the task of rebuilding the monastery. The result was this glorious building where ostentatious display of the Church's power is blended harmoniously with an astute use of space. Don't miss the Emperors' Gallery, and the marble hall with its ceiling by Paul Troger (1732).

Dürnstein (16)
☎ (02711) 375

🕙 *Apr. 1–Oct. 31: 9am–6pm* ● *unaccompanied 20 schillings* 🎫 *every hour, adults 40 schillings, children (6–14) 30 schillings, students 35 schillings.* 📪 🏢

This is the heart of the Wachau, a pretty little town and the setting for another of the region's Baroque gems: the abbey rebuilt in the 1700s on the site of the 15th-century Augustinian monastery. Allow a good half-hour for the climb to the ruins of the old Dürnstein Castle, from where there are magnificent views over the Danube. It was in this castle, in 1192, that Richard the Lionheart, King of England, was held prisoner for some months by Duke Leopold V. The two had quarreled violently during the Siege of Acre, and an unlucky shipwreck forced Richard to return overland through Austria.

Krems (17)
☎ (02732) 85620

The two medieval cities of Krems and Stein – which eventually grew into one – enjoyed early prosperity thanks to the construction in the 15th century of the first permanent crossing over the Danube. The upper town of Krems, with the Hoher Markt and the Gozzoburg, is the hub of the city and the oldest area; lively and business-conscious, it has been restored in exemplary fashion and is largely pedestrianized. Stein, a sleepier place than its neighbor, has preserved its lovely old houses.

Not forgetting

■ **Landhaus Bacher (18)** Mautern ☎ (02732) 82937 🕙 Wed.–Sat. 11.30am–2pm, 6.30–9pm; Sun. 11.30am–9pm *At Mautern, on the opposite bank of the Danube. The kitchen is in the charge of one of the region's most famous women chefs.* ■ **Weingut Jamek (19)** Joching 45, 3610 Weissenkirchen ☎ (02715) 2235 🕙 Mon.–Thu. 11.30am–4pm; Fri. and Sat. 11.30am–9pm.) *A reputed cellar, with excellent food.* ■ **Prandtauerhof (20)** Joching 36, 3610 Weissenkirchen ☎ (02715) 2310 🕙 Tue.–Sat. 11.30am–9.30pm; Sun. 11.30am–3.30pm *Wines, liquors and regional dishes.*

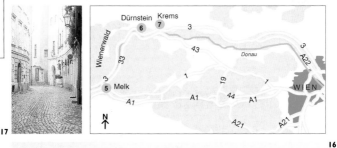

The Wachau has much to offer, with its graceful landscapes, pleasant climate, historic monuments and quality wines.

Store opening times
Except for food stores, the usual opening hours are 9am–6pm
Monday through Friday and 9am–5pm Saturday. Food stores
open earlier (from 7 or 8am) and close later (7 or even 8pm).
In stations, tobacconists, news-stands and snackbars stay open
until around 10.30pm.

➡ Where to shop

Holiday markets

During the weeks
leading up to Easter
and Christmas,
fleamarkets spring up
all over the city. At
Christmas, there are
stalls selling all sorts of
decorations, small craft
objects and goodies to
eat. At Easter, the stalls
around the Freyung are
awash with thousands
of eggs, hand-
decorated in every
color of the rainbow.

Vienna's main shopping areas

The central pedestrianized area, Kärntner Strasse–Graben–Kohlmarkt and the adjacent streets, is also one of the smartest areas in Vienna, where all the famous stores can be found. If you've a passion for shopping, you should also take a walk along Mariahilfer Strasse, Vienna's longest commercial street, with its own host of top names.

56 Stores

THE INSIDER'S FAVORITES

Clothes sizes

Most clothes are sold in standard European sizes, as opposed to the system used in the UK and the USA. There are some exceptions – women's blouses, for instance, are sold in Austrian sizes.

INDEX BY TYPE

In the area
▪➔ **Where to stay:** ➡ 18 ➡ 20 ➡ 22
▪➔ **Where to eat:** ➡ 40
▪➔ **After dark:** ➡ 66 ➡ 70 ➡ 82
▪➔ **What to see:** ➡ 100 ➡ 102 ➡ 108 ➡ 114–115

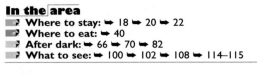

Where to shop

Ringstrassen Galerien (1)
Kärntner Ring 9-13, 1010

Ⓜ *U1, U2, U4 Karlsplatz* **Shopping Mall** 🕐 *Mon.–Fri. 10am–7pm; Sat. 10am–5pm* 📶 🚻 ▨ **Pachisi Toys** *Palais Corso, 1st floor* ▣ ☎ *(1) 512 7150* ➠ *(1) 512 7150-4* **Mala Strana Decoration** *Palais Corso, 1st and 2nd floors* ▣ ☎ *(1) 513 0180* ➠ *(1) 513 0183*

The Ringstrassen Galerien were opened in 1994. The mall extends over 3 buildings linked by walkways, with no less than 70 stores. Two of these merit special attention: Pachisi Toys and Mala Strana Decoration. Pachisi are major specialists in wooden toys, but also stock a vast range of collectable dolls and cuddly animals. Inside Mala Strana Decoration there are hundreds of nooks and corners and display rooms where you can find absolutely anything for the home. There is furniture in every style – classic, ethnic, designer, contemporary – as well as fabrics, objets d'art and crockery. The interior design is stunning, and there is around 10,000 sq ft of floor space. Areas resembling Aladdin's Cave alternate with more elegant rooms where pride of place is given to big tables laid out with fabulous dinner-services. You won't find a better opportunity for thinking about making changes at home!

Arcadia (2)
Kärntner Strasse 40, 1010 ☎ (1) 513 9568 ➠ (1) 513 9886

Ⓜ *U1, U2, U4 Karlsplatz* **Music, photographs** 🕐 *Mon.–Sat. 9.30am–6.30pm; Sun. 10am–6.30pm* ▣

Arcadia can be found under the arcades of the Staatsoper, and specializes in operatic CDs/records and books on the opera. There are also hundreds of photographs of operatic celebrities. Autograph hunters will certainly be in luck here – unless of course they prefer to wait for the divas and famous tenors to emerge from the stage doors, only a step or two away.

Konditorei Sacher (3)
Kärntner Strasse 38, 1010 ☎ (1) 514 56852 ➠ (1) 514 56879

Ⓜ *U1, U2, U4 Karlsplatz* ; *U1, U3 Stephansplatz* **Patisserie** 🕐 *Mon.–Sat. 9am–6pm* ▣ @ http://www.sacher.co.at/sacher

This is where they make the famous *Sachertorte*, the gateau created, as the name indicates, by one Franz Sacher, an apprentice chef at the court of Prince Metternich. Ever since, the recipe has been jealously guarded by the Hotel Sacher, which holds sole rights to sell the one-and-only 'Original *Sachertorte*'. Gourmets rest assured: delivery can be arranged throughout the world! Ask at the Hotel Sacher, Philharmonikerstrasse 4, A-1010 Vienna.

Not forgetting

■ **Da Caruso (4)** *Operngasse 4, 1010 ☎ (1) 513 1326 This is a music store dealing only in classical works. It is just opposite the Staatsoper (Opera) and is a favorite haunt of opera buffs.*

In the area
- **Where to stay:** ➡ 18 ➡ 22 ➡ 26
- **Where to eat:** ➡ 40 ➡ 42
- **After dark:** ➡ 80 ➡ 82
- **What to see:** ➡ 100 ➡ 102 ➡ 108 ➡ 114–115

➡ **Where to shop**

Kunstverlag Wolfrum (5)
Augustinerstrasse 10, 1010 ☎ **(1) 512 5398** ➡ **(1) 125 39857**

Ⓜ *U1, U2, U4 Karlsplatz* **Engravings, books, postcards** 🕐 *Mon.–Fri. 10am–6pm; Sat. 10am–5pm* ▢

A vast choice of engravings and watercolors from the 18th, 19th and 20th centuries – especially Viennese artists from the late 1800s to the early 1900s – framed on the spot at your request.

Michaela Frey (6)
Lobkowitzplatz 1, 1010 ☎ **(1) 513 8009** ➡ **(1) 513 800911**

Ⓜ *U1, U2, U4 Karlsplatz* **Jewelry, accessories** 🕐 ⚅ *Gumpendorferstr. 81, 1060* ☎ *(1) 599250; Vienna Airport* ☎ *(1) 700 73493*

In 1951, Michaela Frey founded a company dedicated to objets d'art. Since her death in 1980, a group of Viennese craftsmen has taken over the business, turning their attention to the production of gold and enamel jewelry (bracelets, brooches, necklaces, rings, earrings, cufflinks, etc.), though they also sell scarves. Nowadays their brand name enjoys an international reputation.

A.E. Köchert (7)
Neuer Markt 15, 1010 ☎ **(1) 512 5828** ➡ **(1) 513 4022**

Ⓜ *U1, U2, U4 Karlsplatz; U3* **Jewelers, watchmakers** 🕐 *Mon.–Fri. 9.30am–6pm; Sat. 9.30am–5pm* @ *aek@koechert.at*

The firm of Köchert were jewelers to the Imperial Court until the fall of the monarchy in 1918. One of their creations was a diamond tiara composed of 27 stars for the Empress Elisabeth; in 1998, on the centenary of Sissi's death, they issued a commemorative replica. Today, Köchert produce new lines in a modern, restrained and elegant style in collaboration with contemporary designers and artists. They have also introduced a range of deluxe watches.

Oberlaa-Stadthaus (8)
Neuer Markt 16, 1010 ☎ **(1) 513 2936-0** ➡ **(1) 513 29360**

Ⓜ *U1, U2, U4 Karlsplatz ; U3 Stephansdom* **Patisserie, chocolates, tearoom** 🕐 *daily 8am–10pm* @ *Stadthaus@Oberlaa-Wien.at, http.www.oberlaa-wien.at* ⚅ **Oberlaa-Babenberg**; *Babenbergerstrasse 7, 1010;* ☎ *(1) 58672820* **Oberlaa-Landstrasse**; *Landstrasser Hauptstrasse 1, 1030;* ☎ *(1) 71527400* **Oberlaa-Am Kurpark**; *Kurbadstrasse 12, 1010* ☎ *(1) 6800 99500*

The first store in this gourmet chain was established at Oberlaa, a small spa on the outskirts of Vienna. Its growing success led to the opening of several branches in the city center. Besides the delicious patisseries, there are specialty chocolates – and for fans of pickled and salted foods, they do a good line in hors d'oeuvres.

Not forgetting

■ **Gebrüder Wild (9)** *Neuer Markt 10-11, 1010* ☎ *(1) 512 5303* *Delicatessen which concocts some good cooked dishes and sells Austrian, Italian and French specialties.*

Köchert has recently reintroduced its diamond stars, beloved of the Empress Sissi.

In the area
- **Where to stay:** ➡ 18 ➡ 22
- **Where to eat:** ➡ 40 ➡ 42
- **After dark:** ➡ 70 ➡ 72 ➡ 78 ➡ 82
- **What to see:** ➡ 108

➡ Where to shop

Lobmeyr (10)
Kärntner Strasse 26, 1010 ☎ (1) 512 0508 ➡ (1) 512 0508-085

🅼 U1, U2, U4 Karlsplatz **Glassware** 🕐 Mon.–Fri. 9am–6pm; Sat. 10am–5pm ▢

Lobmeyr were purveyors of glassware to the Imperial Court, and took pains to employ only the best craftsmen; at the turn of the 20th century, they were working in close collaboration with representatives of the Viennese Secession, such as Adolf Loos. Today their creations are famous worldwide, with their chandeliers hanging resplendent in the City Opera House and in the Metropolitan Opera in New York. The Kärntner Strasse store offers a wide choice of wine glasses, carafes, and particularly champagne glasses, of which they stock 25 different types.

Wolford (11)
Kärntner Strasse 29, 1010 ☎/➡ (1) 512 8731

🅼 U1, U2, U4 Karlsplatz; U1, U3 Stephansplatz **Lingerie; hosiery** ▢ 🕐
@ http://www.wolford.com

When they opened their store in 1946, Wolford made only socks. With the arrival of nylon in Europe during the 1950s, they launched into the production of pantyhose and stockings. Since then, the Wolford label can be found all over the world. Theirs is a deliberately up-market brand – their lines are not cheap, but the quality is first-rate. The present policy emphasizes originality, though not at the expense of elegance.

Steffl (12)
Kärntner Strasse 19, 1010 ☎ (1) 514310 ➡ (1) 513 1650

🅼 U1,U2, U4 Karlsplatz; U1, U3 Stephansplatz **Department store**
🕐 Mon.–Fri. 9.30am–7pm; Sat. 9.30am–5pm ▢ 🏨 ☒ @ steffl@vienna.at

As if an entire renovation of the premises was not enough, Steffl are now dedicated to promoting a new concept in shopping. First, customers telephone to indicate what they want, and the staff select a range of likely items. The final decision is then made at a pre-arranged appointment in a special viewing/trying-on room. This extraordinary level of service is absolutely free. In 2000, a museum of multimedia is due to be opened in the basement. The chosen title is 'Mozart World, Vienna' – recalling the fact that, until the mid-19th century, Mozart's last house stood on the site of the present store. The ground floor is devoted to beauty products; floors 1–4 house men's and women's fashion, including the world's top designer names. The 'Amadeus' area, which occupies the 5th and 6th floors, is given over to books, music and multimedia. Room has also been found for a literary café and a cybercafé. Finally, on the 8th floor, you can take a welcome break in the restaurant or the American bar, with exhilarating views over the rooftops of Vienna and St Stephen's cathedral.

Not forgetting

■ **Prachner (13)** Kärntner Strasse 30, 1010 ☎ (1) 512 85490 *One of the city's largest bookstores, with a wide range of local books.* ■ **Rosenthal (14)** Kärntner Strasse 16, 1010 ☎ (1) 512 3994 *Department store for interior design, dishes and accessories for the home. All leading European brands.*

In the area
- ➔ **Where to stay:** ➜ 22 ➜ 24 ➜ 26 ➜ 28
- ➔ **Where to eat:** ➜ 42
- ➔ **After dark:** ➜ 74 ➜ 78 ➜ 80 ➜ 82
- ➔ **What to see:** ➜ 88 ➜ 92

Where to shop

Theyer & Hardtmuth (15)
Kärntner Strasse 9, 1010 ☎ (1) 512 3678 ➜ (1) 512 5341

Ⓜ U1, U3 Stephansplatz **Pens, stationery, glass and crystal ware**
Ⓞ Mon.–Fri. 9.30am–6pm; Sat. 10am–5pm ▭
@ theyer-hardtmuth@theyer-hardmuth.at

In addition to selling its large range of pens, this store is also the official agent for the Austrian glass and crystal ware manufacturers Swarovski, and stocks their famous miniatures (small animals, musical instruments, cut-glass fruits), plus jewelry (brooches, pendants) and key-rings.

Gmunden (16)
Kärntner Durchgang, 1010 ☎/➜ (1) 512 5824

Ⓜ U1, U3 Stephansplat **Ceramics** Ⓞ Mon.–Fri. 9am–6pm; Sat. 9.30am–5pm ▭

Gmunden is a small town in Upper Austria with the largest ceramics factory in central Europe. Austrians can immediately recognize its distinctive motifs – floral patterns or green stripes. All pieces are hand-painted. There are more than 1,200 different types of ware such as coffee services, vases, pitchers and salad bowls.

Augarten Wien (17)
Stock-im-Eisen-Platz 3, 1010 ☎ (1) 512 1494

Ⓜ U3 Stephansplatz **Porcelain** Ⓞ Mon.–Fri. 9.30am–6pm; Sat. 9.30am–5pm
▭ ◀▶ Schloss Augarten, Obere Augartenstr. 1A, 1020 ☎ (1) 2112418 6,
Mariahilferstrasse 31 ☎ (1) 587 9218 Schwechat airport ☎ (1) 700 733163

All Augarten porcelain is handmade in the best craft traditions. Since its foundation in 1718, the company has always employed the talents of great Viennese artists in its search for new ideas in design and decoration. There are guided tours of the Augarten workshops Monday through Friday at 9.30am. Address: 2, Schloss Augarten, Obere Augartenstrasse 1A, 1020 ☎ (1) 211 2411.

Helmut Lang (18)
Seilergasse 6, 1010 ☎ (1) 513 2588

Ⓜ U1,U2, U4 Karlsplatz; U1, U3 Stephansplatz **Men's and women's fashion** ▭

The Viennese designer Helmut Lang is undoubtedly the world's leader in ready-to-wear fashion. He made his name chiefly through the use of original materials, such as rubber and vinyl. His new collections are strikingly set off by the store's layout and its sober, even stark décor.

Not forgetting
■ **Österreichische Werkstätten (19)** Kärntner Strasse 6, 1010 ☎ (1) 512 2418 Interior design items in glass or metal; handmade jewelry by Austrian craftsmen.
■ **Haban (20)** Kärntner Strasse 2, 1010 ☎ (1) 512 6730 Broad choice of up-market, classic watches (Rolex, Cartier, Chopard...) plus more way-out designer styles.

15

16

17

16

19

The making of porcelain is a centuries-old art in Austria. The acceptance of new ideas has allowed this fine tradition to continue in the 21st century.

18

20

For marriages and other special occasions, Austrians still wear the traditional costume known as *Trachten*. For men this means shirt and jacket plus either long or short pants; women wear a full-skirted dress with a tight bodice and an apron. In winter, the outfit is completed by a green felt hat and a loden overcoat.

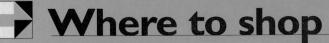

Where to shop

Tostmann & Co (21)
Schottengasse 3a, 1010 ☎ (1) 533 5331 ➠ (1)533 5331-32

Ⓜ *U2 Schottentor* **Traditional costumes** 🕒 *Mon.–Fri. 10am–6.30pm; Sat. 9.30–5pm*

There is nowhere in Vienna to find a better selection of quality *Dirndl* – women's traditional costumes. Colors, motifs and materials are very varied, and you'll find it hard to resist temptation. The store also sells men's and children's clothing, and there is a hire service too.

Lanz (22)
Kärntner Strasse 10, 1010 ☎ (1) 512 2456 ➠ (1) 512 6775

Ⓜ *U1, U2, U4 Karlsplatz; U1, U3 Stephansplatz* **Traditional costumes** 🕒 *Mon.–Fri. 9.30am–6pm; Sat. 9.30am–5pm* ▭

In Salzburg, in 1922, Josef Lang had the idea of adapting the traditional country-style costume to reach a wider clientele, especially in the cities. Here you can find a truly classic outfit – a cotton *Dirndl*, for instance – as well as a wide selection of traditional children's costumes and elegant *Trachten* for men, all of impeccable quality.

Oberwalder & Co (23)
Kärntner Strasse 39, 1010 ☎ (1) 512 2841 ➠ (1) 604 611416

Ⓜ *U1, U2, U4 Karlsplatz; U3 Stephansplatz* **Millinery, souvenirs** 🕒 *daily 9am–7pm; Sat. 9am–5pm* ▭ 🔁 *Mariahilferstrasse 61, 1060*

In the season, Oberwalder sells tourist souvenirs, but its main trade is in

millinery. Why not set off your classic loden headwear with some little accessory: a feather or two or a hunting trophy? The women's hats are really chic: it's by no means rare to see them on the crowned heads of Europe.

Loden Plankl (24)

Michaelerplatz 6, 1010 ☎ (1) 533 8032 ➡ (1) 535 4920

Ⓜ U3 Herrengasse *Traditional costumes, accessories, footwear*
🕐 *Mon.–Fri. 9am–6pm; Sat. 9am–4pm* ▢ @ *loden@plankl.at*

Situated opposite the Hofburg, this is Vienna's oldest store (1880). Here you will discover loden wear in every conceivable form (jackets, coats, sweaters, capes…) and variety (Himalayan loden, silk loden, cashmere loden…). The choice is staggering. You can also buy traditional and hunting-style costumes in cotton or leather, together with accessories: shoes, belts and even underwear.

Not forgetting

▄▄ **Leben mit Tradition (25)** Seilergasse 10, 1010 ☎ (1)512 2241 *Men's and women's clothing, especially traditional styles. The new collections are modern, unostentatious and comfortable.* ▄▄ **Kettner (26)** Seilergasse 12, 1010 ☎ (1) 5132239 *Clothing, footwear and accessories for both sexes. Decidedly classic outfits, often inspired by traditional costumes. Country clothes for hikers and shooters.*

➡ Where to shop

Doris Ainedter (27)
Jasomirgottstrasse 5, 1010 ☎ (1)532 0369

Ⓜ U1, U3 Stephansplatz **Women's fashion** 🕐 Mon.–Fri. 10am–6.30pm; Sat.
10am–5pm ▤ @ ainedter@aon.at 🔼 Marc-Aurelstrasse 4, 1010 ☎ (1) 5335893

The boutique is modern, quietly elegant, and covers some 32,000 sq ft.
Here youthful fashion creator Doris Ainedter unveils her colorful designs
and develops her talent as an image consultant. She starts from the
assumption that while working women generally have little time to buy
clothes or promote their image, appearance plays an ever-increasing role
in their professional lives. Her solution is to employ advisers who help
the identity-conscious customer select the right outfit.

Vinothek St Stephan (28)
Stephansplatz 6, 1010 ☎ (1) 512 6858 ➡ 02236 453705

Ⓜ U1, U3 Stephansplatz **Wines** 🕐 Mon.–Fri. 9.30am–6.30pm; Sat. 9.30am–
1pm ▤

A welcoming environment where you can cheerfully taste a glass or two.
There is a selection of the best Austrian wines, from the Wachau, Lower
Austria, Burgenland and Styria, as well as shelves of foreign imports.

Galerie Nächst St Stephan (29)
Grünangergasse 1, 1010 ☎ (1) 512 1266 ➡ (1) 513 4307

Ⓜ U1, U3 Stephansplatz **Art gallery** 🕐 Mon.–Fri. 11am–6pm; Sat. 11am–4pm
▤ @ http://www.kunstnet.at/st-stephan

From the first days of this gallery in 1954, Otto Mauer devoted himself
to promoting the international avant-garde and establishing contacts
with the major European galleries. Rosemarie Schwarzwälder took over
the reins in 1978, placing the emphasis firmly on Abstract, Conceptual
and Minimalist art. But not just any Tom, Dick or Harry exhibits here;
Rosemarie has her fancies and her blue-eyed boys!

Schönbichler (30)
Wollzeile 4, 1010 ☎ (1) 512 1868

Ⓜ U1, U3 Stephansplatz **Tea, liquors, specialty groceries** 🕐 Mon.–Fri.
8.30am–6pm; Sat. 8.30am.–12.30pm ▤

At the end of a covered passageway linking the Stephansplatz to the
Wollzeile is a store with an immensely impressive frontage. Now this is
really a place to make your mouth water. The teas may have their
reputation, but the whiskeys and other liquors will satisfy the most
demanding palate. As for the other goodies and house specialties,
gourmets and gluttons alike will hit the jackpot.

Not forgetting

■ **Haas & Haas (31)** Stephansplatz 4, 1010 ☎ (1) 512 9770
*Fine assortment of teas and coffees, with an enormous choice of accessories:
containers for tea and coffee, tea balls, candy-sugar sticks, teapots, coffee pots.*
■ **Buchhandlung 777 (32)** Domgasse 8, 1010 ☎ (1) 513 1177
*An esoteric bookstore specializing in astrology. Peaceful and pleasant atmosphere;
large range of titles.*

A whole range of small, unusual, boutiques surround the Stephansplatz.

In the area

➡ **Where to stay:** ➡ 24 ➡ 26
➡ **Where to eat:** ➡ 40 ➡ 42
➡ **After dark:** ➡ 80 ➡ 82
➡ **What to see:** ➡ 92 ➡ 100 ➡ 102 ➡ 108

➡ Where to shop

Braun & Co (33)
Graben 8 ☎ (1) 512 55050 ➡ (1) 512 550584

Ⓜ *U1, U3 Stephansplatz* **Ready-to-wear clothing and accessories**
🕐 *Mon.–Fri. 10am–6pm; Sat. 9.30am–5pm* ▯

At the corner of the Graben and Spiegelgasse (The Street of the Mirror)
is the district's most chic boutique, founded in 1892. Its wooden front
has bow windows which set off the garments like jewels in display-cases.
The inside is no less striking; everything is in wood – superb pieces of
old furniture replace traditional racks, highlighting top international
brands of ready-to-wear fashions for both sexes. The service is all you'd
expect; each customer is met and assisted by expert members of the
sales team.

Altmann & Kühne (34)
Graben 30, 1010 ☎ (1) 533 0927 ➡ (1) 216 5402

Ⓜ *U1, U3 Stephansplatz* **Confectioners** 🕐 *Mon.–Fri. 9am–6.30pm;
Sat. 10am–5pm* ▯

This confectionery store can be found in an Art-Nouveau block on the
Graben. It was already a favorite in the days of the monarchy and has
remained faithful to the traditions of the past. Only specialist production
staff are employed; the work is long and painstaking, especially when
making 'Lilliputs', the house specialty. These are tiny candies sold in
delightful, distinctively shaped presentation boxes resembling chests of
drawers, treasure chests, and so on.

Rasper & Söhne (35)
Am Graben 15, 1010 ☎ (1) 53433 ➡ (1) 533 8037

Ⓜ *U1, U3 Stephansplatz* **Interior design, crockery, glassware** 🕐 *Mon.–Fri.
9.30am–6pm; Sat. 10am–5pm* ▯ @ *rasper-soehne@netway.at*

The principal trade of this establishment is in an Austrian brand of wine-
glass familiar to connoisseurs and wine lovers the world over: Riedel.
After consulting leading wine experts, Claus Riedel became the first to
produce glasses designed to bring out the best qualities of wine. Today
the *Sommelier* collection boasts thirty different types all produced at the
Kufstein factory, opened in 1756.

Döblinger (36)
Dorotheergasse 10, 1010 ☎ (1) 515 0322 ➡ (1) 515 0351

Ⓜ *U1, U3 Stephansplatz* **Music** 🕐 *Mon.–Fri. 9am–6pm; Sat. 9am–noon*

Vienna's biggest music store sells books, sheet music, teaching manuals,
CDs and occasionally, for collectors, autographs and original scores.
There is also a second-hand department.

Palmers (37)
Graben 14, 1010 ☎ (1) 532 4058

There are dozens of lingerie stores in Vienna. The Palmers chain – with
over seventy branches in the city – is the best known. Its stores can be
recognized by their gold and green sign.

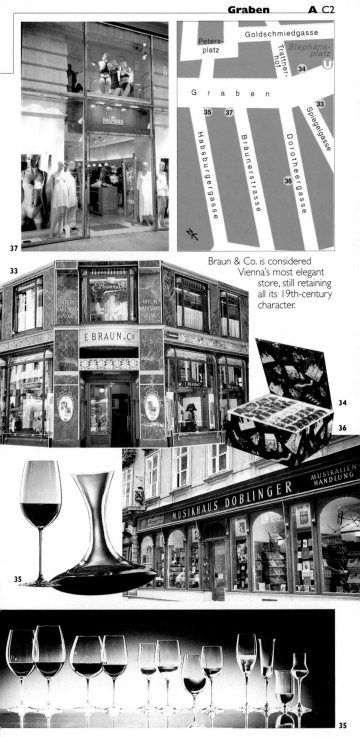

Braun & Co. is considered Vienna's most elegant store, still retaining all its 19th-century character.

37

33

34

36

35

35

In the area
- **Where to stay:** ➡ 26
- **Where to eat:** ➡ 40 ➡ 42 ➡ 46
- **After dark:** ➡ 80 ➡ 82
- **What to see:** ➡ 92 ➡ 100 ➡ 102

➡ Where to shop

Ch. Demel's Söhne (38)
Kohlmarkt 14, 1010 ☎ (1) 535 17170

Ⓜ *U3 Herrengasse* **Confectionery, patisserie, tearoom** Ⓞ *Mon.–Fri. 10am–7pm* ▢ ⬛

Demel's patisserie, dating from 1786, is a real institution in Vienna. You'll find it hard to resist the temptation to stay for tea and try out their confections in the elegant surroundings. The house specialties are presented in deluxe boxes specially designed for Demel by the Wiener Werkstätte group in the early 20th century.

Thonet (39)
Kohlmarkt 6, Postfach 36, 1010 ☎ (1) 533 7788 ➡ (1) 533 778877

Ⓜ *U3 Herrengasse* **Interior design** Ⓞ *Mon.–Fri. 10am–6pm; Sat. 10am–5pm* ▢

Can there be anyone who hasn't heard of the famous Chair No. 14 created by Michael Thonet (1796–1871) in the 1850s? More than 50 million copies had been sold when production ceased in 1930. Meantime, it had helped furnish cafés and hotels the world over. Today, at the Kohlmarkt store, you can buy a replica of No. 14 – as well as of other traditional or modern lines, all simple, functional and elegant – in kit form. The firm's success has been based on close collaboration with the best designers of each period, such as Adolph Loos and Otto Wagner at the turn of the 20th century or Le Corbusier in the 1930s.

Haider-Petkov (40)
Kohlmarkt 11, 1010 ☎ (1) 533 2005

Ⓜ *U3 Herrengasse* **Women's fashion** Ⓞ *Mon.–Fri. 11am–6pm; Sat. 11am–5pm* ▢ ⬛ *Wollzeile 6, 1010 ☎ (1) 533 2005*

All the clothes sold under this label are in a form of knitwear manufactured and sewn like cloth. Customers can order garments made-to-measure, with a choice of designs and colors. Two trends stand out in the new collections: a lightweight knit, based on materials like mohair, which lends the creations a spider's-web delicacy, and a tighter knit using materials with a metallic look but still soft to the touch.

Not forgetting

■ **Schullin & Seitner (41)** Kohlmarkt 7 ☎ (1) 533 9052 *A store designed by the architect Hans Hollein in 1982. Sells jewelry blending traditional and contemporary idioms.*
■ **Meinl am Graben (42)** Graben 19 ☎ (1) 532 3334 *Vienna's largest stockist of food and specialty groceries. Besides necessities they sell Austrian specialties (such as charcuterie and beers) and unusual items.*
■ **Pots & Pieces (43)** Neglergasse 9 ☎ (1)533 8678 *This small store on the Naglergasse – a pretty little pedestrianized street leading from the Graben to the Am Hof Square – deals in crockery (pottery and porcelain), decorative candles, lamps and table linen. Most of the products are handmade.*

41

Bognergasse

Naglergasse

43   42   Graben

39

Wallnerstrasse

41

Haarhofg.   Irisg.

Fahneng.

38

Herrengasse

Kohlmarkt

40

Michaeler-
platz

Tuchlauben

41

43

Julius Meinl

40

38

40

39

In the area
➡ **Where to stay:** ➡ 26 ➡ 30
➡ **Where to eat:** ➡ 46 ➡ 48
➡ **After dark:** ➡ 68 ➡ 80 ➡ 82
➡ **What to see:** ➡ 94 ➡ 96 ➡ 98 ➡ 114–115

➡ Where to shop

Henn (44)
Naglergasse 29, 1010 ☎ (1) 533 83820 ➡ (1) 533 8673

Ⓜ *U3 Herrengasse* **Interior design** ▱

This is a first-class interior design store with nearly 5,000 sq ft of floor space spread over two stories. Furniture, lamps, fabrics, accessories, novelty items and gadgets by internationally acclaimed contemporary designers, including Austrians. You can also take a mini world tour among the numerous ethnic objects from Africa and Asia.

Katze & Kater (45)
Palais Ferstel, Herrengasse 14/Freyung 2, 1010
☎ (1) 535 4372 ➡ (1) 533 6297

Ⓜ *U3 Herrengasse* **Gifts** 🕐 *Mon.–Fri. 10am–6.30pm; Sat. 10am–5pm* ▱

Katze & Kater have the largest collection of cat figures in Europe: some 2,500 of them. They come in ceramics, wood, bronze, glass or metal, mostly handmade, and at a more than reasonable price, being imported directly from the country of origin without the intervention of wholesalers. An ideal store to find a little gift for the children, and maybe their parents too.

Kaufhaus Schiepek (46)
Teinfaltstrasse 3, 1010 ☎/➡ (1) 533 1575

Ⓜ *U2 Schottentor ; U3 Herrengasse* **Costume jewelry, beads** 🕐 *Mon.–Fri. 10am–6pm; Sat. 11am–5pm* ▱

A jewel-box indeed. This little store is overflowing with thousands of beads of every shape, size, and color – wooden beads, metal beads, rock beads, plastic beads, glass beads. You can all make the necklace of your dreams! If you lack the creative impulse, try the ready-made jewelry – it's very original. There's also a great choice of attractive buttons.

U.u.M. Beschorner (47)
Schottengasse 2, 1010 ☎ (1) 533 1428 ➡ (1) 406 334621

Ⓜ *U2 Schottentor ; U3 Herrengasse* **Gloves, scarves** 🕐 *Mon.–Fri. 10am–6pm; Sat. 10am–5pm* ▱

You will spot this store way down the Schottengasse by its handsome sign. Founded in 1854, this is the oldest glover's in Vienna. Gloves of every sort, in every material; classic or modern designs for men or women, and a good selection of scarves.

Not forgetting

■ **Einwallwer Workshops (48)** Palais Harrach, Freyung 3
☎ (1) 535 3730. *These consist of two stores facing each other in the delightful inner courtyard of the Palais Harrach. Objets d'art and a quality range of traditional and modern furniture.*
■ **Tao (49)** Schottengasse 3 ☎ (1) 535 8856. *Small boutique: ready-to-wear women's outfits by Austrian couturiers.*

Connoisseurs of fine furniture and antiques should make sure they visit the delightful little city-center streets like the Stahlburgasse, Habsburgergasse, Dorotheergasse, or Bräunerstrasse, which form the hub of the antiques trade. But if it's secondhand bargains that set your adrenaline flowing, head straight for the fleamarkets.

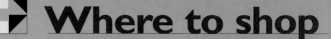

Where to shop

50

51

50

Flohmarkt am Naschmarkt (50)
Wienzeile, 1050 ☎ **(1) 546 34430**

🅼 *U4 Kettenbrückengasse* **Craft items, secondhand goods** 🕒 *Sat., except public holidays, 6.30am–6pm.*

Vienna's biggest and most famous *flohmarkt* is held in back of the Naschmarkt – the city's great food market. Both major antiques dealers and small secondhand dealers trade here, not to mention private individuals selling every conceivable item. Best arrive early to avoid the crowds of sightseers.

Dorotheum (51)
Dorotheergasse 17, 1010 ☎ **(1) 515600** ➡ **(1) 515 60443**

🅼 *U1, U2, U4 Karlsplatz* **Auction rooms** 🕒 *Mon.–Fri. 10am–6pm; Sat. 9am–5pm* 🔲

The emperor Joseph I established a pawnbroker's store on this site; the interest obtained from loans was directed to charitable causes. Nowadays the Dorotheum is the setting for some 650 auctions a year – pictures, antiques of all periods and styles, jewelry, carpets and rugs, musical instruments, toys, old books … As a result, it has become the world's sixth largest auction house.

Glasgalerie Michael Kovacek (52)
Spiegelgasse 12, 1010 ☎ **(1) 512 9954** ➡ **(1) 513 2166**

🅼 *U1, U3 Stephansplatz* **Glassware** 🕒 *Mon.–Fri. 9.30am–6pm; Sat. 9.30am–12.30pm* 🔲

An outstanding collection of glassware of all periods and styles. There are displays on two floors.

Antiquitäten D & S (53)
Dorotheergasse 13, 1010 ☎ (1) 512 5885 ➡ (1) 512 588575

M U1, U3 Stephansplatz *Furniture, clocks* 🕐 Mon.–Fri. 10am–6pm; Sat. 10am–1pm (closed Sat. in summer) ▢

The window display is always fascinating, with its highly impressive collection of Biedermeier clocks and mantelpiece ornaments. Don't be afraid to walk in: there are some superb pieces of 18th- and 19th-century furniture – Baroque, Empire and Biedermeier – inside.

Not forgetting

■ **Kunst und Antiquitäten Markt Am Hof (54)** Am Hof, 1010 ☎ (1) 531 14431 🕐 March–Christmas, Fri., Sat. 10am–7pm. *Small market with 30–40 stallholders. Objets d'art, craft stands, books and miscellanea.* ■ **Kunst und Antiquitäten Markt am Donaukanal (55)** Donaukanal, ☎ (1) 531 14431 🕐 May–Sep., Sat. 2pm–8pm; Sun. 10am–8pm. *On the banks of the Danube canal, old city side, between the Augarten and Aspern bridges. Secondhand and craft stalls.* ■ **Bric-à-Brac (56)** Habsburgergasse 9, 1010 ☎ (1) 533 6026 ➡ (1) 53360265 🕐 Mon.–Fri. 11am–6pm; Sat. 10am–midday. *Absolutely anything: countless odds and ends, from an old movie theater seat to a teddy bear via secondhand books.*

Finding your way

The districts of Vienna

Vienna is divided into 23 districts (*Bezirke*); these form a spiral around District no. 1, which is also known as the *Innere Stadt* – literally the Inner City, the historic central area contained within the Ringstrasse.

Best foot forward!

The 'Inner City' boasts a checkerboard of pedestrianized zones (Kohlmarkt, Graben, Stephansplatz, Kärntner Strasse...), public transport is frequent and comfortable, and the attractions are relatively close together on and inside the Ring. What better excuse to make use of your own two feet?

6
Maps

Understanding place names

Bezirk: district
Brücke: bridge
Garten: garden
Gasse: small street
Graben: street on site of ancient defensive ditch
Markt: market
Platz: square, place
Ring: Vienna's peripheral road (UK: ringroad; US: beltway)
Schloss: castle, royal residence
Strasse: street
Tor: gate
Ufer: riverbank, shore

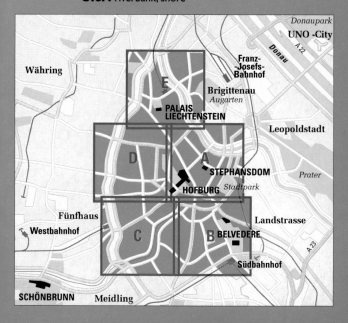

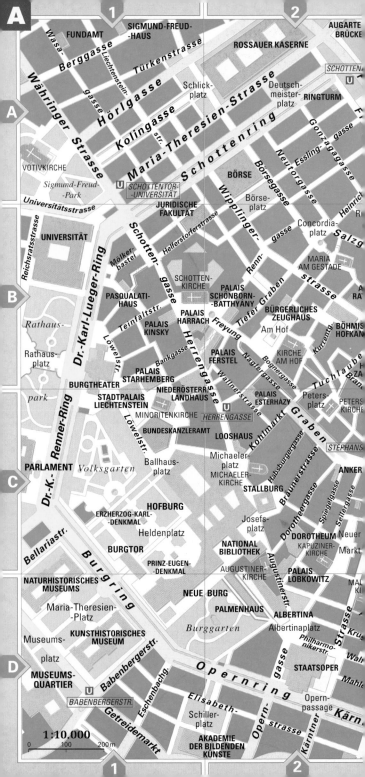

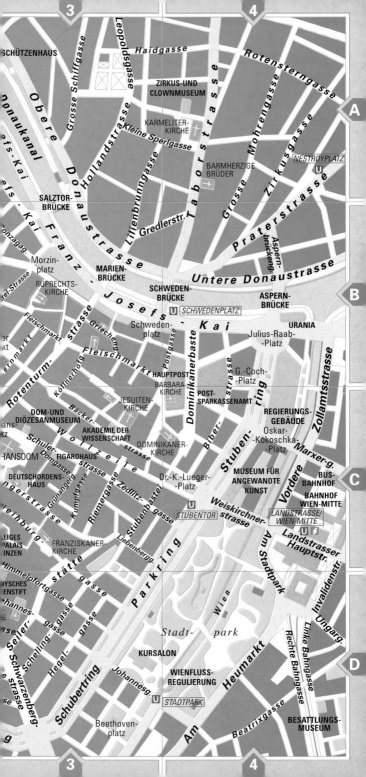

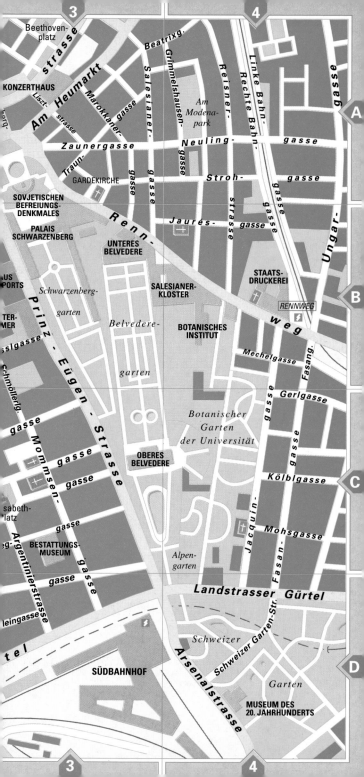

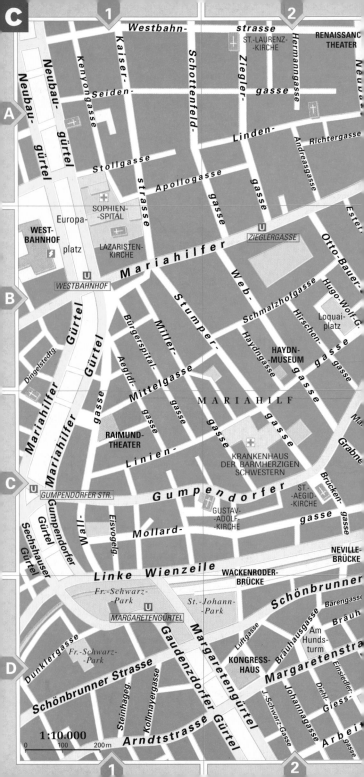

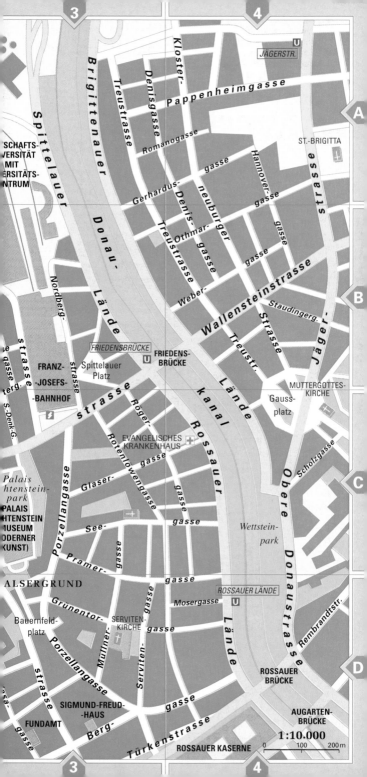

Streets are listed in alphabetical order. The first letter – in bold – after each entry is the serial letter of the map; the other letters and the figures denote the grid reference.

Street
index

Subway plan

Key

- $U1$ Subway line (U-Bahn)
- $S1$ Schnellbahn line (S-Bahn)
- Vienna-Baden railway
- Bus station
- Information point
- Airport

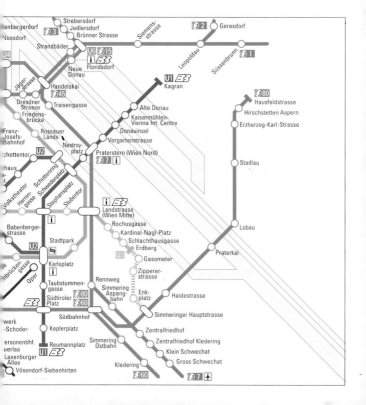

All practical information, advice, and useful numbers concerning travel to and around Vienna will be found in the Getting there section on pages 6–15.

General
index

The publishers wish to thank Brigitte Resch, the Austrian Tourist Office, and Österreich Werbung (Ö.W.) for their invaluable assistance in preparing this guide.

Picture
credits

1 and front cover ill. Donald Grant **2** Nelson (K. Schiefer); G. Jung (E. Bakos) **6** M. Bassi **8/9** M Bassi;Y. Boehmer (Hilton terminal) **10/11** Y. Boehmer; Holzbachova/Bénet (Vienna sign) **12/13** Y. Boehmer; M. Bassi (subway interior, streetcar, carriage driver); Ö.W. Haider (Balhaus Platz sign) **14/15** M. Bassi; Y Boehmer (telephone card, bills and coins, dispenser, postal and pharmacy signs) **16** Ana Grand Hotel **19** 1, 4, 5, 6 Y. Boehmer; 2 Hotel Bristol; 3 Hotel Astoria/Holan **21** 7 Ana Grand Hotel; 8 Imperial; 9 Hotel am Schubertring (exterior); Y. Boehmer (interior) **23** 10 Ambassador (interior), Y. Boehmer, 11, 14 Y. Boehmer; 13 Pension Aviano **25** 15, 18 Y. Boehmer; 16 Kaiserin Elisabeth; 17 Hotel am Stephansplatz (reception), Hotel am Stephansplatz/W. Knorr (bedroom interior) **27** 19, 20, 21, 22 Y. Boehmer; 23 Pension Pertschy im Palais Cavriani **29** 24, 28 Y. Boehmer; 26 Radisson SAS Palais Hotel; 27 Vienna Marriott **31** 29 Austria; 30 Kärntnerhof; 33 Y. Boehmer **33** 35 Hotel im Palais Schwarzenberg; 36 Hilton Vienna; 37 Y. Boehmer; 38 Inter-Continental Wien; 40 Starlight Suite Hotel **35** Y. Boehmer **37** 47 Altstadt; 48 K +K Hotel Maria Theresia; 49, 51 Y. Boehmer; 50 Astron Suite Hotel

38/41 Y. Boehmer **43** 5, 6, 7, 10 Y. Boehmer; 9 Weibels Bistro **45** Y. Boehmer **47** 15 Bei Max; 16, 17 Y. Boehmer; 18 È Tricaffè **49** Y. Boehmer **51** 23, 25 Y. Boehmer; 26 Y. Boehmer (interior), Ö.W./Wiesenhofer **53/55/57/59/61** Y. Boehmer **62/63** 47 Kierlinger; 49 Mayer am Pfarrplatz; 50 Oppolzer; 51 Zimmerman **64** Ö.W./ Bartl **67** 1 Ö.W./ Bartl (stage), Österreichischer Bundestheaterverband/ A. Zeininger; 2 Ö.W./ Trumler; 4 Österreichischer Bundestheaterverband/ A. Zeininger; 5 Y. Boehmer **69** 6 M. Bassi; 7, 8 Y. Boehmer; 9 Vienna's English Theater/Inter-Thalia (ceiling), Y. Boehmer. **71/73/75/77/79** Y. Boehmer **81** 43, 44, 45, 47, 50 Y. Boehmer; 46 Ö.W./Bartl **83** 51 Ö.W./Kalmar (interior), Y. Boehmer; 52, 53, 54 Y. Boehmer **84** WFVW/Wiesenhofer **86/87** Ö.W./Grossauer (Dr.-K.-Lueger-Ring), Ö.W./ Bartl (Haas-Haus and Stephansdom), M. Bassi (Secession Building, carriage in the Hofburg), Ö.W/Mayer (Michaelertor) **89** 1 Ö.W./Bohnacker (top), TCI Archives, M. Bassi (bottom); 2 TCI Archives; 3 Y. Boehmer **91** 6, 7, 9 Y. Boehmer; 8 Ö.W./Wiesenhofer **93** 11, 12 Y. Boehmer; 13 M. Bassi (fountain), Ö.W./Mayer (square), Ö.W./Trumler (door) **95** 15 TCI Archives; 16 Y. Boehmer; 17

Ö.W./Mayer, Y. Boehmer (Anchor Clock); 19 WFVW **97** 20, 23 Y. Boehmer; 21 TCI Archives; 22 Y. Sacquépée (statues), Y. Boehmer; 24 M. Bassi **99** 25, 26 M. Bassi; 28 Ö.W./Mayer; 29 Y. Boehmer **101** 30 J. Da Cunha (apartments: interior), Lessing/Magnum (imperial treasure), Ö.W./Wiesenhofer (salon); 32 Y. Boehmer; 33 ÖFVW **103** 34 TCI Archives, ÖFVW (riders entering), M. Bassi (stables: exterior); 36, 37 Ö.W./Trumler (interior), ÖNB (sphere) **105** 38 M. Bassi; 39 Kunsthistorisches Museum (entrance), TCI Archives; 40 Naturhistorisches Museum **106/107** 42 Y. Boehmer; 43, 47 TCI Archives; 45, 46 M. Bassi **109** 48 TCI Archives; 49, 50 (Albertina: facade) M. Bassi; 50 TCI Archives; 51 Ö.W./Trumler **111** 52 TCI Archives; 53 Y. Boehmer (museum: facade), TCI Archives; 54 Schubert Haus; 55 Y. Boehmer **113** 56 M. Bassi; 57 Direktion der Museen der Stadt Wien; 58 Ö.W./Wiesenhofer (Belvedere: exterior), TCI Archives **114/115** 60 M. Bassi, Y. Boehmer (Johann Strauss statue); 61 M. Bassi (statue), Y. Boehmer; 62 M. Bassi; 63 Y. Boehmer **117** 64 Ö.W./Markowitsch; 65 M. Bassi; 66 Ö.W./ Mayer (Lusthaus), Ö.W./Diejun; 67 Ö.W./Wiesenhofer **119** 69 Ö.W./Wiesenhofer (Schönbrunn: exterior), TCI Archives; 70 TCI Archives; 71 Ö.W./ Mayer (Gloriette); Ö.W./ Wiesenhofer **120** Ö.W./Camiel 128 Gmunden **131** 1 Ö.W./Kalmar (interior), Pachisi Toys, Y. Boehmer (Mala Strana Décor); 2, 4 Y. Boehmer; 3 M. Bassi (sign), Sacher **133** 5 Micaela Frey,

Y. Boehmer (exterior); 6, 8, 9 Y. Boehmer; 7 A.E. Köchert, Y. Boehmer (sign) **135** 10, 11, 13 Y. Boehmer; 12 Steffl, Y. Boehmer (mannequin); 14 Rosenthal **137** 15 Theyer & Hardtmuth; 16 Gmunden; 17, 18, 19 Y. Boehmer; 20 Haban/Lorenz **138/139** 21, 22, 23, 24 Y. Boehmer; 25 Y. Boehmer (interior), Leben mit Tradition **141** 28, 30, 31, 32 Y. Boehmer; 29 Galerie Nächst St. Stephan **143** 33, 36, 37 Y. Boehmer; 34 Altmann & Kühne; 35 Rasper & Söhne/Riedel Glas **145** 38, 39, 41, 43 Y. Boehmer; 40 Haider-Petkov; 42 M. Bassi **147** 44 Henn/Der Bunte Elephant/Simone; 45 Katze & Kater; 46 Kaufhaus Schiepek; 47, 49 Y. Boehmer; 48 Einwaller Workshops **148/149** 50 M. Bassi, Y. Boehmer (jars); 51, 52, 53, 54 Y. Boehmer **150** M. Bassi